FAITH, REASON, AND SKEPTICISM

FAITH, REASON, AND SKEPTICISM

Essays by

WILLIAM P. ALSTON

ROBERT AUDI

TERENCE PENELHUM

RICHARD H. POPKIN

Edited and with an Introduction by

MARCUS HESTER

ıple University Press / Philadelphia

Temple University Press, Philadelphia 19122
Copyright © 1992 by Temple University. All rights reserved
Published 1992
Printed in the United States of America

LIBRARY OF CONGRESS
CATALOGING-IN-PUBLICATION DATA
Faith, reason, and skepticism / essays by William P.
Alston . . . [et al.] ; edited and with an introduction by
Marcus Hester.
     p.   cm.—(James Montgomery Hester seminar ;
8th (1989))
     "The 8th James Montgomery Hester seminar."
     ISBN 0-87722-853-1 (hard)
     1. Religion—Philosophy—Congresses.   I. Alston,
William P.   II. Hester, Marcus B.   III. Series: James
Montgomery Hester seminar ; 8th.
BL51.F32 1991
200'.1—dc20   91-8835

CONTENTS

FAITH, REASON, AND SKEPTICISM

INTRODUCTION

William Alston opens this dialogue on faith, reason, and skepticism by arguing that if the belief-forming processes of a typical Christian are reliable, one can *know* particular religious claims such as that Jesus was the incarnation of God. Particular religious claims differ from knowledge of the general claims of natural theology such as that God exists, and Alston's investigation necessarily involves traditional and recent concepts of epistemology. Much of this tradition has centered on the view that knowledge is justified true belief, and Alston's analysis centers on the nature of this justification.

A view of justification especially prominent since Descartes is internalism, defined by Roderick Chisholm as: "If a person is *internally justified* in believing a certain thing, then this may be something he can know just by reflecting on his own state of mind."[1] The chief problem of an internalist epistemology, as Alston sees it, is that it cannot connect justification to truth. Alston argues instead for an epistemological view that is primarily externalist. Externalism is a rejection of internalism. It specifically means a person can be justified in the conversions of true belief to knowledge even if he or she cannot formulate these conditions of justification. Reliabilism is a version of externalism that states that a belief is reliably produced if it is produced in a way that generally produces true beliefs. Reliabilism illustrates the naturalization of epistemology through the study of belief-forming mechanisms that tend to produce truths. Even though Alston states that he has a theory of justification, his discussion of the reliableness of particular Christian beliefs does not use or need this theory. The subject of justification can deflect attention from the main thrust of reliabilism.

Suppose a Christian believes God is loving because the Bible and church say He is. Then if these two sources are reliable in producing truths, the Christian *knows* God is loving even if he or she cannot say why these truths are reliable. Knowing that p is different from knowing why one knows p. "What these appeals [to the Bible and church] do presuppose is that God is at work in the composition and transmission of the Bible and in the life of the church in such a way as to render them by and large reliable sources of belief about the central concerns of the faith." But, to the despair of the unbeliever, just as empirical (perceptual) studies are necessary to show perception itself to be a reliable belief-producing mechanism, so the reliableness of these sources (the Bible, the church, and God's grace) depends on theological considerations. It is admitted that the latter is circular, but all epistemology is circular, contrary to what a pure internalist such as Descartes thought.

Robert Audi contrasts faith with belief, especially with what he calls "flat-out belief"—belief that is unqualifiedly believing a proposition, as opposed to such things as believing it probable, believing it certain, half believing it, believing it conditionally. Thus he develops the concept of what he calls "nondoxastic faith." Using the Greek word *doxa* for belief, nondoxastic faith means faith that is distinct from beliefs held with the certainty of flat-out belief. The contrast between faith and belief is hard to see if one concentrates only on propositional faith, such as that God exists, in contrast to attitudinal faith, such as faith in God. His essay thus "explores the possibility that a religious commitment, with faith as its central element, can be rational even if theistic beliefs, particularly the kind philosophers have defended by argument, should turn out not to be." His strategy is twofold: to emphasize ways in which faith is a distinct attitude and to give faith a greater role in considerations of the rationality of religious commitment. Nondoxastic faith has cognitive and noncognitive dimensions and in fact may have the same propositional content as full belief. Thus, Audi does not think he is driven to reduce faith to a noncognitive attitude.

Audi emphasizes nondoxastic faith partially because he has doubts about the sort of nonmystical, experiential justification of belief in God advocated by neo-Calvinists such as Plantinga. Audi devotes more than two sections to the analysis and criticism of this neo-Calvinistic concept of experience.

Audi argues both that the criteria for rationality of faith and hope are less stringent than those for flat-out beliefs and that rationality itself is a less stringent concept than justification. "Rational faith is epistemically less at risk than rational belief." Nondoxastic faith at least satisfies the criteria of rationality. Even though some Christians may have justifiable belief, and even flat-out belief, some Christians have faith that is not belief. And Christians who have faith only do not necessarily think it less likely that, say, God is sovereign than do Christians who have justified belief. A Christian with nondoxastic faith may be as intense and certain, with a certainty based on hope, as a doxastic Christian. (Yet Audi later suggests that such faith is "far from conclusive.") He is not, however, advocating fideism, since he defends at least the *rationality* of nondoxastic faith.

Terence Penelhum argues that defenses of religion cannot be made in the same way as defenses of beliefs of common sense. Religious beliefs have competitors (religious pluralism or multiple religious ambiguity) in a way commonsense beliefs do not. Both Pascal and Hume saw that Pyrrhonian skepticism does not lead to peace of mind, but Hume's solution is common life in which natural instincts are reinforced. Pascal would deny that such diversions of social life are a solution. Instead, we must conquer our wretchedness by opening our heart to God in faith. For both Hume and Pascal, natural instinct is an antidote, but not an answer, to skepticism. Hume advocates a beliefless conformity to 'philosophical religion' divorced from the excesses of the religious enthusiasts or evangelicals of his time. I take it that Audi would not want to equate his nondoxastic faith to the beliefless conformity to harmless religious rituals of a Sextus Empiricus and perhaps even of a Hume.

Thomas Reid, alone among these thinkers, thought belief in God, unlike commonsense beliefs, needed a justification by natural theology; and Penelhum develops and defends this point of view instead of the solutions of Pascal, Nicholas Wolterstorff, Alston, and Alvin Plantinga. Plantinga and Wolterstorff have argued that belief in God does not need a proof of the sort given by natural theologians since such belief is properly basic in the sense that it is properly basic to believe in external objects and other minds. And contrary to Alston's emphasis on religious experience, Penelhum argues that religious experience of competing religions only increases the uncertainties of religious pluralism. Penelhum claims that these thinkers may succeed in showing that it is rational to hold religious beliefs without the independent support of natural theology, but they cannot deal with multiple religious ambiguity. "Parity is not enough." Thus natural theology is urgent. Traditionally, natural theology did not show just that belief in God is rational but that its denial is irrational. It is irrational to deny that which can be proved about God. Penelhum does include under natural theology more and different premises than the usual general truths about the world available to all men, such as, "It is certain and evident to our senses that in the world some things are in motion." Natural theology is natural, not because its premises can be known to everyone, "but because they can be known to be true without already knowing or believing that God exists, and without any grounding in experience of God." Natural theology, as conceived of by Penelhum, can include historical reports, events known or experienced by the hearer or reader, and even alleged miracles.

Successful natural theology would eliminate the excuse of unbelief because of the lack of reasons for belief in God and would throw into sharper focus other possible explanations of unbelief such as sin. I cannot tell if the disambiguation Penelhum promises from natural theology, as he conceives of it, would distinguish one religion from another, say Christianity from Islam, or merely disambiguate the religious from the secular. His solution cannot really help with "multiple religious ambiguity" unless it does the former, and perhaps there is little hope that it can do this.

Penelhum's essay will be of interest to those who approach

problems in philosophy of religion in a contemporary, analytic way and to scholars of Hume, Reid, and Pascal.

Richard H. Popkin argues that the use of skepticism in the seventeenth and eighteenth centuries, say that of Montaigne and Pascal, is not incompatible with religious faith. Skepticism was used to attack the certainty of dogmatic religious claims, both Christian and Jewish, and was meant to lower dogmatists' certainty so faith and miracles would be more believable. Some of the Jewish use of skepticism to criticize Christian claims anticipated modern Biblical criticism. For Popkin, these criticisms have neutralized "questionable metaphysical theology" of Jews, Christians, and Moslems and have left us with creedless and institutionalless mysticism and spirituality.

The essays that follow were read at the eighth James Montgomery Hester Seminar, held at Wake Forest University April 14 and 15, 1989. This seminar is endowed by a generous gift from James Montgomery Hester, a 1917 graduate of Wake Forest, in honor of Dr. A. C. Reid, beloved teacher and long-term chairman of the Department of Philosophy.

Marcus Hester
Wake Forest University

Note

1. Roderick Chisolm, *Theory of Knowledge*, 3d ed. (Englewood Cliffs, N.J.: Prentice-Hall, 1988), p. 7.

William P. Alston

1

KNOWLEDGE OF GOD

I. The Intuitive Conception
and Knowledge of God

In this essay I shall explore the possibilities for knowledge of God that are opened up by recent developments in epistemology that go under the title *externalism;* more specifically, I shall be concerned with the version of externalism known as *reliabilism.* I shall set this up with a consideration of how those possibilities look from a more internalist epistemological stance. I shall be working from within the Christian tradition, though I take my remarks to have a wider bearing.

It is a familiar view that knowledge of God—His nature, doings, and purposes—is either nonexistent or very restricted, and that, at least for the most part, believers have to make do with faith rather than with knowledge.[1] This view has been widely held by both friend and foe of religious belief, and it goes back many centuries. A classic statement is found in Aquinas. Although the existence and certain basic features of the nature of God can be known in the strict sense, everything else in the Christian faith must be accepted on faith, which he defines as "the assent of the intellect to that which is believed" where this is "not through being sufficiently moved to this assent by its proper object [in which case it would constitute knowledge], but through an act of choice, whereby it turns voluntarily to one side rather than to the other." Faith is distinguished from opinion by the fact that it involves "certainty and no fear of the other side."[2] In modern times the view has been enthusiastically endorsed

6

by such diverse fideists as Pascal, Kant, and Kierkegaard, but its acceptance has been much wider, including, on the side of believers, such figures as F. R. Tennant and Paul Tillich. Needless to say, unbelievers deny any knowledge of God; we will attend to some of them shortly. Deliberately distorting the terms for my own use, I shall refer to those who hold that we can have knowledge of God as *gnostics* and those who deny this as *skeptics*. I shall set aside questions about the meaningfulness, consistency, coherence, and other internal features of religious belief, taking it that all parties to the discussion agree that beliefs about God constitute genuine candidates for knowledge, if only the right further conditions are satisfied.

Whether we can have knowledge of God depends on what knowledge is, and varying positions on this have been taken in the history of philosophy. Throughout most of that history, the dominant conception has been what we may cal the *intuitive* conception. Knowledge, to quote a particularly succinct twentieth-century formulation, is "simply the situation in which some entity or some fact is directly present to consciousness."[3] Various forms of this conception are to be found in Plato's conception of the awareness of Forms, Descartes's notion of "clear and distinct perception," and Locke's definition of knowledge as the "perception of the agreement or disagreement of ideas,"[4] as well as Aquinas's insistence that for any knowledge that goes beyond sense perception, the object must be intellectually "seen," that is, as directly presented to the intellect as a seen object is to vision.[5] Many contemporary epistemologists take this notion to be intolerably obscure; nevertheless, I think that paradigm examples like simple, self-evident truths of mathematics and logic tie down the notion sufficiently to enable us to see that articles of the Christian faith like Creation, the dealings of Jahweh with Israel, the Incarnation, and the Trinity are not strong candidates for being directly presented to the mind in this way. To be sure, the proponents of this conception of knowledge recognize that a fact may be known not only by being itself directly presented to awareness but also by being logically derived from such truths. That leaves open the possibility that some articles of faith might be demonstrated from premises that are directly presented to awareness, but, by almost common consent, this is a live possibility for a few such articles at most, and the usual contemporary view is that it extends to none.

This denial of knowledge of God is only as cogent as the conception of knowledge on which it is based, and that conception has virtually disappeared from the epistemological scene. One factor in this is disillusionment about the concept of direct *awareness, presentation,* or *givenness* of facts,[6] though, as indicated above, I find this reaction to be overblown. It is true that, by the nature of the case, no satisfactory analysis can be given of the notion of direct awareness, but it is only an unfounded dogma that every respectable concept must justify that title by the provision of an analysis; analysis must start somewhere, and why not here? A more serious disability is the drastic restriction on the extent of knowledge that this conception enforces. Very little of what we take ourselves to know can lay claim to be "directly present to consciousness." The past and future, the distant in space, generalizations of all sorts, hypotheticals, the unobservable fine structure of things, all fall outside this area. Knowledge is restricted to self-evident truths, our own conscious states, perhaps what we directly perceive in the external environment, and what can be deductively derived from this. Thus H. A. Prichard:

> . . . we are forced to allow that we are certain of very much less than we should have said otherwise. Thus, we have to allow that we are not certain of the truth of an inductive generalization, e.g., that all men are mortal, or that sugar is sweet, for we are not *certain* that anything in the nature of man requires that he shall at some time die; we are not even certain that the sun will rise tomorrow . . . It is of no use to object, "Well, if you are going to restrict what we know to what we are certain of, you are going to reduce what we know to very little." For nothing is gained by trying to make out that we know when we do not. . . .[7]

But we are forced to recognize that we do not know any of these things only if we adopt a conception of knowledge as restrictive as this one, and that is just the question.

II. *The Justified-True-Belief Conception and Knowledge of God*

In this century, at least in English-speaking circles, the assessment of the possibility of religious knowledge is more likely to be conducted against the background of a conception of knowledge as *justified true belief* (JTB). Whereas the intuitive conception took knowledge and belief to be mutually exclusive psychological states (belief being the *supposition* that a fact obtains, as contrasted with *seeing* that it obtains, having the fact directly presented to one's awareness),[8] the JTB view regards knowledge as a belief that passes certain tests, namely, truth and justification. Clearly this requires a different conception of belief as well as of knowledge. The JTB conception works with a more neutral account of belief, one that can be briefly indicated by saying that a sufficient condition for a normal mature human being, S, to believe that p is that S would give a positive response to "Is it the case that p?" provided S were disposed to be candid and cooperative.[9] This condition will be satisfied whether S knows or "merely believes" that p.

Before exploring the use of a JTB conception of knowledge in the rejection of knowledge of God, we ought to note the general acceptance of Edmund Gettier's demonstration of the insufficiency of these conditions for knowledge in his celebrated article, "Is Justified True Belief Knowledge?"[10] Contemporary versions of the theory always include one or more additional conditions designed to forestall Gettier counterexamples. I shall ignore this complication in the sequel, since the attacks on religious knowledge in which I am interested are all designed to show that the putative knowledge in question fails to satisfy the justification condition.

Let me also say a word as to how we should understand 'justification' for purposes of this discussion. (Here I speak not of the *conditions* for justification, which I will discuss at length, but of what justification *is,* how we are to conceive that for which the alleged conditions are conditions.) The major divide here is between those who do and those who do not take being justified in believing that *p* to consist in some sort of "deontological" status, for example, being free of blame for believing that *p* or having satisfied one's intellectual obligations in doing so. The nondeontologists will generally take justification to be some other sort of evaluative status, for example, being based on an adequate ground.[11] In the works cited in note 11, I give reasons for rejecting any version of a deontological concept, on the grounds that they either make unrealistic assumptions of the voluntary control of belief or they radically fail to provide what we expect of justification. Hence, I will be thinking in terms of some nondeontological evaluative conception. I may as well go with my favorite: "being based on an adequate ground."[12] As we shall see, it fits nicely into the arguments given by our contemporary skeptics.

In looking at twentieth-century skeptics, I am going to concentrate on nonbelievers. The main reason for this is that they are more thoroughgoing in arguing for their skepticism. Believing skeptics are primarily concerned with working out a viable alternative stance toward the articles of faith. They tend to quickly concede that knowledge is impossible and pass on to their main task of depicting what we have instead. The unbeliever, on the other hand, is confronted with no such task, and takes his main job to be demolishing pretensions to knowledge of God.

As a background for this consideration, let us fill out a bit more the Thomistic picture of the situation. Certain basic propositions concerning the existence and nature of God can be demonstratively proved on the basis of premises that are known with certainty. For other articles of faith, we can produce supporting considerations that make it rational to accept the thesis that their truth is vouched for by the authority of God, though this support is not of such a magnitude as to compel rational assent. The considerations in question appeal to evidences of the divine

authority (divine guidance) of the Bible and the church. They include miracles, prophecies, and the growth of the church.[13] Our
contemporary skeptics attack both parts of the Thomistic scheme.
They seek to show that alleged proofs of the existence and nature
of God lack cogency, and they argue that the "evidences" of revelation are much too weak to do the job. Just to pick two names out
of a vast crowd, this is the sort of thing we find in such works as
God and Philosophy[14] and The Presumption of Atheism[15] by Antony
Flew and The Miracle of Theism[16] by J. L. Mackie.[17]

To have something relatively specific to work with, let us leave
to one side the existence, omnipotence, and omniscience of God,
and other standard theses of natural theology, and concentrate
on a distinctively Christian thesis like the Incarnation. Let us say
that the average Christian believes that God became man in Jesus
Christ to save us from sin and death (if you prefer some other
statement of the purpose, fill that in as you see fit) because this
is asserted in the Bible, by Jesus and others, or because it is proclaimed by the church. Our skeptics will take this to be a radically
insufficient reason for the belief—radically insufficient to render
the belief justified; and since knowledge requires justified belief,
this is enough to prevent the believer from knowing this, even
if the belief is true. What basis do they have for this judgment?
To spell this out adequately, we will have to go into their background epistemology, and to accomplish that, we will have to do
a lot of digging. Unlike Aquinas, the likes of Flew and Mackie do
not put their epistemological cards on the table. I will not have
time for close textual exegesis. I will have to content myself with
plausible conjectures that I am confident could be supported by
further scholarship.

First, we will have to decide whether they are more coherentist
or foundationalist. Here I will just say that they certainly do not
sound like coherentists. In any event, if they are proceeding on
a coherentist basis, the game is up already, both because of the
fatal disabilities to which coherentism is heir and because of the
fact that beliefs about God seem to do as well as anything else on
a coherentist epistemology.[18] I will assume that they presuppose

some kind of foundationalism (the exact brand does not matter) and proceed accordingly.

On a foundationalist epistemology, what does it take for a belief to be justified? Broadly speaking, there are two possibilities. A belief can be *indirectly* or *mediately* justified, justified on the basis of (by the mediation of) other justified beliefs; or it can be *directly* or *immediately* justified, justified on the basis of something other than that. Experience is one major alternative. What gives foundationalism its distinctive thrust is that (1) it recognizes direct as well as indirect justification, and (2) it holds that all indirect justification traces back eventually to directly justified beliefs. Now remember that we are working with a conception of justification as being based on an adequate ground. Thus, if a belief in the Incarnation is to be justified, it must be either based on adequate reasons, in the shape of other things one knows or justifiably believes (indirect justification), or based on something else, for example, on experience, in the way beliefs about one's current conscious states are, and, depending on one's views of the epistemology of perception, in the way one's belief that one sees a tree directly in front of one is (direct justification). As for the latter, contemporary skeptics typically take it as obvious that no religious beliefs can be directly justified. This view has been recently challenged both by Alvin Plantinga[19] and by me.[20] Indeed, it is challenged by the entire mystical tradition. This is not to say that every religious belief can be reasonably thought of as justified by one's experience of God, but neither can it be taken as obvious that no religious beliefs can be directly justified. However, since I have other fish to fry in this essay, I will not contest the point here. I will concede for the sake of argument that if a belief about God is to be justified, the belief will have to be held on the basis of adequate reasons. We must now consider what is required for that.

JTB theorists are by no means in agreement on this, but I believe that an account of the sort I am going to present is widely accepted, and that it is something like this account that lies behind the skeptics' claim that such reasons as Christians have for

their beliefs are insufficient to do the job. Let us say, then, that
S's belief that p is based on an adequate reason, q, iff:

1. S believes that q.
2. S is justified in believing that q.[21]
3. S believes that p because he believes that q.[22]
4. q provides adequate support for p.[23]
5. S knows, or justifiably believes, that q provides adequate
   support for p.
6. S would cite q in justification of his belief that p if challenged.[24]

Let us apply this account of mediate justification to the question of whether it is possible for someone to be mediately justified
in believing that Christ died as an atonement for our sins, where
the person, S, believes this on the ground that it is asserted by
Saint Paul or that it is a dogma of the church. We can stipulate
that conditions 1, 3, and 6 are satisfied.[25] That is, S believes as
he does because of certain reasons and is quite aware that he
does so. He has access to the reasons on which his belief depends and he regards those reasons as sufficient. In such cases
the claim of the critic is that conditions 2 and 4 cannot both be satisfied. In this instance, for example, condition 2 may be satisfied
if the reason is simply that Saint Paul or the church asserts this.
There is no particular difficulty in S's being justified in supposing
that. But then condition 4 (and hence condition 5) is not satisfied. The mere fact that the thesis is propounded by that person
or that institution is not a sufficient reason for accepting it. We
lack sufficient reasons for supposing that Saint Paul or the church
authorities have such expertise in theological matters that their
pronouncements are a reliable guide to the truth. To be sure, to
go into these matters, we would have to examine the traditional
"evidences" of the authority of the apostles and of the church and
determine whether they are sufficient to shore up the claims they
are invoked to support. But since I am primarily interested in exploring the prospects of knowledge of God on a quite different
approach to knowledge, I will just accept the critic's judgment

on these points and agree that no one has sufficient reason for supposing that condition 4 is satisfied in this instance (and hence that no one satisfies condition 5). To be sure, if q were beefed up to include the proposition that the Bible is the word (message) of God to us or that the church is guided by the Holy Spirit in its doctrinal pronouncements, it would be a different story. Now it will be universally agreed that the reason provides adequate support. Surely God (the Holy Spirit) is an authority on theological matters! But now the critic will deny that S is justified in accepting this enriched premise and deny this for essentially the same reasons for which he denied that condition 4 is satisfied for the original premise. Just as we lack sufficient reason for supposing that the mere fact that p is asserted by Saint Paul or the church is a sufficient reason for believing it, so we lack sufficient reason for supposing that the Bible is the word of God or that the church is guaranteed by God to be correct in its doctrinal pronouncements. If we had sufficient reason for the latter, we would ipso facto have sufficient reason for the former.[26]

So let us agree that, by the standards of this epistemology,[27] Christians are never justified in their distinctively Christian beliefs about God, and hence that, even if those beliefs are true, none constitutes knowledge. Whether this should disturb Christians depends on the credentials of this epistemology, a matter to which I now turn.

III. Internalism

The most obvious problem facing a JTB conception of knowledge, and indeed facing any theory of justification, is a methodological one: How do we determine what conditions are sufficient for justification? (Now we are considering what, in particular, is required for justification, not how the concept of justification is to be understood.) In a foundationalist theory, this divides into two questions: (1) How do we tell what suffices to render a belief directly justified? and (2) How do we tell when a reason provides adequate support for a belief (adequate grounds for taking the belief to be true)? These are very large questions, and here I will be able only to indicate the most important difficulties confronting JTB theorists in this area.

One approach to these issues has to do with likelihood of truth. After all, whatever else epistemic justification of beliefs may be, it is clearly supposed to be a commodity that is valuable from the standpoint of the search for truth, for the aim at restricting our beliefs to what is true. This suggests that a belief counts as justified only if it is at least likely to be true and, more specifically, that what justifies a belief thereby renders it likely to be true.[28] And that suggests in turn that at least part of what is required if a condition C is to suffice to justify belief B is that the process of forming B on the basis of C is a reliable one, one that can be counted on to lead to truth, at least most of the time. So if we want to know whether a belief that there is a tree in front of me is justified by virtue of being based on a certain kind of visual experience, what we need to consider is whether the process of belief formation exemplified by forming that belief on the basis of that kind of experience is a reliable one, one that can be depended on to (usually) yield true beliefs. And if we want to know whether the belief that the generator is not functioning properly is justified by virtue of being based on my knowledge that a certain portion of the dashboard has lighted up, we must consider whether beliefs like that are reliably formed on the basis of facts like that; in other words, we must consider whether such a light is a reliable indication of a defective generator.

But the trouble with this, a trouble that, among other things, has inhibited most epistemologists from proceeding in this way to determine what justifies what, is that we cannot settle these questions about reliability without relying on principles of justification that are of the same sort as those we are trying to establish. How do we tell whether a visual experience of type V is a reliable indication of there being a tree in front of me? We certainly have to use empirical evidence to do so, which means that we have to suppose ourselves to be justified in holding a number of beliefs about the environment on the basis of perceptual experience.

And how do we tell that a certain light is a reliable indication of a defective generator? Again, by empirical investigation that will involve assuming, in many cases, that we can form a justified belief on the basis of like indications. Hence, we can never get started on such investigations, at least not without circularity. We have to make use of some principles of justification, at least assume them in practice, to establish any of them in this fashion.

Hence, most theorists of justification have shied away from looking to considerations of reliability to determine what justifies what, and they have taken another route. They have supposed that such determinations can be made, at least in the most basic cases, by rational reflection, just by carefully considering the matter, by "armchair thinking." Let us call this approach *internalism*, using the term in one of the ways it is used in contemporary epistemology.[29] Thus Roderick Chisholm:

> Now, I think we may characterize the concept of "internal justification" more precisely. If a person S is *internally justified* in believing a certain thing, then this may be something he can know just by reflecting upon his own state of mind. And if S is thus internally justified in believing a certain thing, can he also know, just by reflecting upon his state of mind, that he is justified in believing that thing? This, too, is possible— once he has acquired the concept of epistemic justification.[30]

On this "internalism," justification is something of which we can have a priori knowledge, just by thinking about the matter. Like intuitionism in ethics, the view comes in two versions: general and particular. According to the former, we are capable of discerning the truth of general principles of justification by reflection. According to the latter, a more popular form with contemporary internalists including Chisholm, what we can discern on reflection is that a particular belief is or is not justified.[31] We can then arrive at correct general principles of justification by determining which principles best accommodate particular facts of justification.

Thus, to return to our focal concern with Christian beliefs, a

skeptic who is an internalist JTB theorist, closet-variety or otherwise, will suppose that he can determine just by careful reflection
that, for example, introspective and perceptual beliefs are justified when formed in the usual way, and that beliefs formed by
valid deductive or sound inductive inference from justified premises are thereby justified. But he will report that even on the most
careful scrutiny he cannot see that a belief is justified by virtue
of being asserted in the Bible or by the church, unless the credibility of these sources has been established on the basis of beliefs
that, like those just mentioned, can be seen on reflection to be
justified.

IV. Troubles with Internalism

Once again, this denial of knowledge of God is only as compelling as the epistemology on which it is founded; and what are
we to say about that epistemology? There are serious reasons for
being suspicious of internalist justification theory, and hence of
an internalist JTB account of knowledge. The most fundamental
weakness of internalism is its indeterminacy and arbitrariness.
First, consider the particularistic variety. Just what is the status of
the conviction that a particular belief in particular circumstances
is or is not justified? Reflecting on the sharp divergencies in such
convictions among philosophers, an unsympathetic observer will
suspect that these judgments often reflect the theoretical prepossessions of the one who is judging. Am I justified in believing that
there is a tree in front of me when I take, or would take, myself
to suppose that I see a tree in front of me, in the absence of any
reasons for this? Chisholm would say yes; those who stress the
need for discursive support for perceptual beliefs—C. I. Lewis,
Wilfrid Sellars, Laurence Bonjour—would say no. Does the mere
fact that I believe something that is not contradicted by the sum
total of my other beliefs render me somewhat justified in believing it? Some will reply in the affirmative and others in the
negative. And so it goes. This is too easy a way out, too easy a
way to put the stamp of rational acceptance on one's predilec-

tions. Where this approach does seem to yield definite results, this only reflects the fact that most of us are predisposed to agree about the conditions under which certain kinds of beliefs are to be approved. And intuitionism with respect to general principles of justification seems even less promising. Can I ascertain just by reflection the conditions under which perceptual judgments are justified? Again, a consideration of sharply differing positions on the epistemology of perception may well lead us to skepticism about this.

Insofar as mere reflection does seem to yield definite and relatively uncontroversial results, it yields far too little to cover knowledge that it seems for all the world as if we possess. Perhaps we can determine just by thinking about the matter that beliefs about one's current conscious states and beliefs in simple self-evident truths of logic and mathematics are ipso facto justified. But it is dubious that the justificatory status of anything else is clearly revealed to an unclouded inner gaze. In fact, those who have taken intuitionism most seriously in epistemology from Descartes on have generally supposed that the most one can see to be justified immediately in the area of sense perception, for example, is that one is currently having such and such sensory experiences; the existence and nature of anything external will have to be established by argument. It is too well known to require mention that the chief burden of Western philosophy from Descartes on has been the task of "proving the existence of the external world." Those who have sought to evade this task, from Reid to G. E. Moore and H. H. Price, have, while taking (some) perceptual beliefs to be immediately justified, definitely not claimed an intuition of the truth of any such principle of justification. Instead they have defended it as a principle of commonsense[32] or a reasonable assumption[33] or the only alternative to skepticism.[34] The lack of intuitive assurance for any principles of inductive logic has been, if anything, even more generally recognized since the time of Hume. Thus if we rely on intuitionism we will be in danger of ending up with a basis of private experience and deductive logic—a basis far too meager to yield anything like the extent of knowledge it seems clear that we possess.

Some internalists have sought a firmer basis for principles of justification than the "bare intuition" envisaged by such thinkers as Chisholm, while still preserving the a priori character of our knowledge of justification. One suggestion is that what suffices for the justification of beliefs in a certain range is determined by the concepts used in beliefs of that range. The idea goes back to Wittgenstein's insistence on "criteria" for the application of concepts. A prominent contemporary exponent, who stresses the epistemological bearing of the view, is John Pollock.

> To learn the meaning of a concept . . . is to learn how to use it, which is to learn how to make justifiable assertions involving it. . . . the meaning of a concept is determined by its justification conditions.[35]
>
> The justification conditions are themselves constitutive of the meaning of the statement. We can no more prove that the justification conditions of "That is red" are the justification conditions than we can prove on the basis of something deeper about the meaning of "bachelor" that all bachelors are unmarried . . . the justification conditions of "That is red" or "He is in pain" are constitutive of the meanings of those statements and hence cannot be derived from any deeper features of their meanings. There are no deeper features.[36]

Thus, we can know, just by reflecting on the concepts involved, what it takes to justify any particular belief. And this holds open the promise of an internalist validation of principles of justification.

There are various difficulties in supposing that all, or almost all, of our concepts are made up of justification conditions, but in this brief discussion I will confine myself to the following point. If justification conditions are to make up even part of my concept of a tree, then obviously I must have the concept of justification. And it seems clear that the least sophisticated humans who have the concept of a tree, like very small children, lack any such concept of justification. A two-year-old child knows what doors and windows, birds and dogs, trees and bushes, adults and children look like, and he can recognize them perceptually; hence, he has concepts of these objects. But it would be rash to suppose that the two-year-old can wield a concept of being epistemically justified in a belief. Of course one does not have to be able to express a concept verbally to have it; but it is highly dubious, at best, that a two-year-old child has a concept of epistemic justification even in a tacit, "practical employment" form. And once we recognize that one can have a usable concept of a dog or a tree without any justification conditions figuring in that concept, we are led to wonder whether the presence of such conditions in more sophisticated concepts, if they are present, has the epistemological consequences Pollock draws. Pollock supposes that it is conceptually impossible for us to fail to be justified in believing that there is a tree in front of us when we have the right kind of sensory experience (in the absence of reasons for thinking the situation to be abnormal), and that we can realize this to be the case just by reflecting on our concept of a tree. But once we see that it is always possible to retreat to a more primitive concept that is like the (untechnical) adult concept except for embodying no justification conditions, we must consider whether we should use the more rather than the less sophisticated concept.[37] And that, at bottom, is just the question of whether the justification conditions involved, by hypothesis, in the adult concept, are, in fact, required for justification. We have not really answered that question by noting that our adult concepts embody an answer to it. We are still left with the question of whether that is the correct (warranted, reasonable) answer. The appeal to the constitution of concepts has gotten us nowhere.

Finally, if one despairs of an a priori grasp of objective facts of justification but still feels tied to internalism, one may seek to subjectivize justification in one or another way. Maximal subjectivity (whatever one thinks justifies a belief does so) has not been popular, but a more qualified subjectivism has been given powerful expression by Richard Foley in his recent book *The Theory of Epistemic Rationality*.[38] On Foley's position it is epistemically rational for a person to believe that *p* "just if he has an uncontroversial argument for p, an argument that he would regard as likely to be truth preserving were he to be appropriately reflective, and an argument whose premises he would uncover no good reasons to be suspicious of were he to be appropriately reflective."[39] Contrary to appearances, this formulation does not rule out immediately justified beliefs; a belief is immediately justified when the argument in question has the sole premise that the subject believes that *p*. Now Foley's view is certainly sufficiently subjectivist for it to be possible that the justification conditions for a given kind of belief are radically different for you and me, in case there are radical differences in what we would judge about arguments on appropriate reflection. Foley believes that there is considerable convergence in the population, but that is not part of the position. But an account of justification that allows for such individual differences does nothing to support the skeptics' cause. If they were to adopt that account, they would be powerless in the face of a believer who, on adequate reflection, would take himself to have an uncontroversial argument for the Incarnation. Hence, a position like Foley's can be of no use for the skeptic.

Thus, an internalist account of justification, of the sort under consideration, faces considerable, even fatal, difficulties of its own, quite apart from any problems that specifically concern the religious sphere; and these difficulties are inherited by an account of knowledge that features internalist justification as a prominent component. When we take justification to be a matter that is to be ascertained, if at all, a priori, by mere reflection, we find our faculties to be unequal to the job of yielding unequivocal, assured results—much less results in sufficient quantity to cover the territory. And this is the case, whichever of the modes of a priori knowledge we think is appropriate to knowledge of justification: synthetic, with Chisholm and others, or analytic, with Pollock and others.

Next I want to note a way in which this internalism constitutes a limitation on the powers of these attempts to determine the conditions of justification, even if we waive the criticisms already aired. The limitation becomes apparent the moment we ask the question, "Can we use these techniques to validate the procedure of forming beliefs on the basis of reflection (rational intuition, reflection on concepts)?" The project of certifying perceptual, memorial, or inferential justification by rational reflection seems attractive just because it avoids epistemic circularity. But that advantage is conspicuously lacking when it is rational reflection itself we seek to ratify. So, at most, the internalist approach would enable us to validate all sources of justification save one, at the cost of taking the credentials of this source for granted. Once we look at the matter in this way, we are struck by a certain arbitrariness in the procedure. Why should we take the justificatory efficacy of reflection for granted, while insisting that the credentials of other sources must be ratified by the use of the former? Is there any justification for this partiality? Thomas Reid saw this point with stunning clarity and gave it powerful expression.

> The author of the "Treatise of Human Nature" appears to me to be but a half-skeptic. He hath not followed his principles so far as they lead him; but, after having, with unparalleled intrepidity and success, combated vulgar prejudices, when he had but one blow to strike, his courage fails him, he fairly lays down his arms, and yields himself a captive to the most common of all vulgar prejudices—I mean the belief of the existence of his own impressions and ideas.
>
> I beg, therefore, to have the honour of making an addition to the skeptical system, without which I conceive it cannot hang together. I affirm, that the belief of the existence of impressions and ideas, is as little supported by reason, as that of the existence of minds and bodies. No man ever did or could offer any reason for this belief. Descartes took it for granted, that he thought, and had sensations and ideas; so have all

his followers done. Even the hero of skepticism hath yielded this point, I crave leave to say, weakly, and imprudently. . . . what is there in impressions and ideas so formidable, that this all-conquering philosophy, after triumphing over every other existence, should pay homage to them? Besides, the concession is dangerous: for belief is of such a nature, that, if you leave any root, it will spread; and you may more easily pull it up altogether, than say, Hitherto shalt thou go and no further: the existence of impressions and ideas I give up to thee; but see thou pretend to nothing more. A thorough and consistent skeptic will never, therefore, yield this point.

To such a skeptic I have nothing to say; but of the semi-skeptic, I should beg to know, why they believe the existence of their impressions and ideas. The true reason I take to be, because they cannot help it; and the same reason will lead them to believe many other things.[40]

The skeptic asks me, Why do you believe the existence of the external object which you perceive? This belief, sir, is none of my manufacture; it came from the mint of Nature; it bears her image and superscription; and, if it is not right the fault is not mine: I even took it upon trust, and without sus-picion. Reason, says the skeptic, is the only judge of truth, and you ought to throw off every opinion and every belief that is not grounded on reason. Why, sir, should I believe the faculty of reason more than that of perception?—they came both out of the same shop, and were made by the same artist; and if he puts one piece of false ware into my hands, what should hinder him from putting another?[41]

Even though the context of Reid's discussion is different from ours in that he is reacting to Humean skepticism, the "undue partiality" point he is making so sharply is the one I am con-cerned to make here. Just as Hume and Descartes were exhibiting arbitrary partiality in taking knowledge of one's own impressions and ideas, plus deductive reasoning, for granted, while requiring that all other claims to knowledge be validated on the basis of the former, so one exhibits arbitrary partiality in taking the justificatory efficacy of rational reflection for granted, while requiring all other putative sources of justification to display their credentials to the former.

Finally, there is a general disability of all these internalist approaches. Even if the argument should be otherwise successful, it would fail to establish claims to justification in a sense of 'justification' that carries a likelihood or presumption of truth. It would fail to show that, for example, normal perceptual beliefs are justified in a truth-conducive sense of 'justification'. Suppose that certain cases of justification are intuitively evident to us on inspection. Does that suffice to show that those beliefs are thereby likely to be true? How could it? How could the fact that certain claims to justification are intuitively evident have any implications as to the likelihood of the truth of ordinary perceptual beliefs or of the conclusion of ordinary inductive inferences? How can we hope to determine the details of reality, even probably, just on the basis of what strikes us as intuitively evident? If we do have such intuitions, by far the most plausible account of what it is those intuitions tell us about is justification in some sense on which the fact that one is *justified* in holding a given belief has no logical implications, even probabilistic ones, for the truth value of that belief. Likewise, even if our concepts do contain 'justification conditions', does that have any implications as to the conditions under which they are (likely to be) truly applied? If so, I could easily determine the conditions under which there is likely to be a war, say, just by building justification conditions of the appropriate sort into my concept of war! Finally, it is even more ridiculous to suppose that if I would on sufficient reflection take there to be an uncontroversial argument for a belief, then that belief is likely to be true. Would it not be megalomaniac to suppose that my inclinations are as potent as that? To be sure, these remarks hold only on a realist conception of truth, according to which the truth of a statement is solely a matter of whether things are as they are therein stated to be, and not a function of our epistemic situation vis-à-vis that statement.[42] On a nonrealist account of truth, according to which, for example, a statement is true if and only if it passes the strongest tests for rational acceptability, it is a different ball game. But that is not really truth.[43]

I take this lack of truth conducivity to be a serious disability of these internalist theories of justification. After all, what gives epistemic justification its distinctively epistemic character is the fact that it is a desirable condition for a belief relative to the basic epistemic goal of maximizing true beliefs and minimizing false beliefs. If a belief's being justified has no implications for the likelihood of its being true, then this is epistemic justification in name only.

I take it that we have exhibited serious deficiencies in an internalist account of justification, and hence in an internalist JTB theory of knowledge. The justification that our skeptics take to be required for knowledge, and that they take to be missing from beliefs about God, turns out to be something other than advertised. First, it suffers from internal weaknesses: it contains insufficient guidelines for its own application, and it fails to exhibit the kind of relation to truth needed for full-blooded epistemic justification. Second, quite apart from religious matters, commonsense principles of justification for, for example, perceptual and memory beliefs lack a solid rationale. The principles that are grounded fall far short of what is needed, or there seems to be an ineluctable arbitrariness in what is claimed to be justified, or, worse, it is dubious that any principles at all get established. Finally, the internalist approach is partial at best; it fails to yield any noncircular justification of its own chosen procedure of rational reflection or intuition.

V. Externalism

All this should motivate us to take a new look at the nature of knowledge. Perhaps we should rethink the idea that knowledge requires justification, internalistically construed. Perhaps this requirement is a millstone around the neck of epistemology, rather than a beacon of light that illuminates the subject matter. This idea is embodied in the contemporary epistemological movement known as *externalism*. Externalism is the denial of internalism; it essentially involves the lifting of the internalist constraint. The externalist holds that it is possible for something to convert true belief into knowledge without the subject's being aware on reflection, or even being capable of becoming aware on reflection, that it possesses this epistemic efficacy. To be sure, we formulated internalism as a constraint on justification, and so a direct denial would be the thesis that conditions could serve to justify without the subject's being able to recognize that on reflection. And some externalists do put their position in this way.[44] But others are not concerned with justification. They make a more radical break with internalist JTB theory and leave justification out of the analysis of knowledge altogether. They provide an externalist substitute for justification in the analysis; the most popular substitute is *reliability*. But even if justification is left out of the account of knowledge, the externalist can still be said to have lifted the internalist constraint on what is required (along with handling Gettier problems) to convert true belief into knowledge, however that is otherwise construed.

In this essay I will focus on reliabilism, construed as the view that knowledge is *true reliably engendered belief*—again, with some additional condition(s) to take care of Gettier problems.[45] Justification will be ignored altogether, as far as the analysis of knowledge is concerned; though I have no tendency to deny that most, or perhaps even all, of our knowledge does involve justified belief.[46] As an initial purchase on the relevant idea of reliability, I will just repeat an earlier statement. To say that a belief is reliably produced is to say that it is produced in a way that can generally be relied on to produce true beliefs.[47] I will develop this position in my own way, but first I will make a few general points that apply to all forms of externalism.[48]

1. Externalism is strongly committed to truth conducivity, the idea that what makes true belief into knowledge is something that will (or would) generally produce true rather than false beliefs. To be sure, the epistemic desirability of truth conducivity

is generally recognized, but what we discovered in the previous section was that internalism sacrifices truth conducivity to intuitive recognizability where they conflict, as is often the case, whereas externalism is prepared to sacrifice intuitive access to truth conducivity. It is a question of priorities. On any version of externalism, a belief will not count as knowledge unless there is something about the way in which it is engendered that renders it at least highly likely to be true.

2. As the last remark suggests, externalists hold that how a belief is produced is crucial for its epistemic status. Actually this is an issue on which internalists are divided, some taking the source-relevant position just outlined, others holding that a belief is justified provided the believer *has* sufficient supporting grounds, whether or not the belief is formed *on the basis of* adequate grounds.[49] But externalists are resolutely committed to the epistemic importance of source.[50]

3. Much of the history of epistemology has been shaped by attempts to respond to skepticism, to show, in the face of skeptical challenges, that we do have genuine knowledge. This may be largely responsible for the pervasiveness of the internalist approach. It has been widely supposed that if I can ascertain in a particular instance whether I really do know just by reflection (intuition), skepticism can get no foothold. This idea may be challenged, as it was by Descartes when he took it that he had to invoke the omnipotence and goodness of God to lay the spectre of skepticism with respect to "clear and distinct perceptions"; but the idea has undoubtedly been powerfully influential. Externalists, on the contrary, show little interest in combatting skepticism. They typically take the attitude that knowledge (justified belief) is a subject matter that is there to be studied like any other, and that there is no more need to prove the existence of knowledge before developing a theory thereof than there is to prove the existence of plants before developing botany. This is one respect in which externalism is sometimes considered a "naturalistic" approach to epistemology.[51]

4. Connected with the previous point is the fact that internalist

and externalist thinking is shaped by radically different models. The background picture for the internalist is that of the highly sophisticated, reflective person who is concerned to subject his beliefs to critical scrutiny, to determine which of them pass the relevant tests for being justified or for counting as knowledge. Roughly speaking, a belief can not count as justified (as knowledge) unless such a person could be satisfied that it does—hence the internalist demand for accessibility of epistemic statuses to reflection. The background picture for the externalist, by contrast, is that of the unsophisticated human or animal perceiver, or even a nonsentient recording device like a thermometer, that is receiving or registering information in a reliable fashion, whether or not it is aware that it is doing so, and whether or not it is even capable of raising the question of whether it is doing so. Assuming that such unsophisticated subjects do acquire knowledge, the externalist would seem to be on strong ground in shaping a conception of knowledge that will accommodate them as well as their more sophisticated brethren.

5. For externalism, knowledge that one knows something is much more dependent on other knowledge than is the case for internalism. On the latter position, much of what is needed to determine that a belief is a case of knowledge can be acquired without dependence on other things we know, since we can tell, just by reflection, when a belief is justified. This point can not be pushed all the way, for truth is also required, and for most candidates for knowledge, no one would suppose that the truth value of the belief can be directly intuited. This is the case for all beliefs about the physical world and other persons. However, for externalism not only truth but also what takes the place of justification cannot be determined without relying on other things the subject has learned about the world. On a reliabilist position, the belief counts as knowledge only if the way in which it was acquired is one that is generally reliable, and that is something that one cannot determine just by turning one's attention to the matter. If it is a perceptual belief, it is a question of how reliable are the perceptual belief-forming mechanisms involved, and that

is a question, broadly speaking, for psychology, physiology, and physics. If it is a belief formed by inference, there is, in addition to issues about the way the premises were acquired, the question of whether the principles of inference involved are such as to yield mostly true conclusions from true premises; and, at least for principles of inductive inference, this cannot be determined by armchair thinking. Roughly speaking, what it takes, on reliabilism, to have knowledge in a given area, and whether a particular belief has what it takes, must be determined in the light of what we know about that area. This point is closely connected with (3). Since I can not know whether and when I have reliable belief about the physical world without relying on knowledge of the physical world to do so, it is obviously hopeless to try to meet the skeptical challenge by constructing a noncircular demonstration of the existence of such knowledge. Thus, externalism is quite prepared to countenance epistemic circularity in attempts to show that we have knowledge or to determine the conditions under which we have knowledge.[52]

Now I want to point out the ways in which externalism in general, and reliabilism in particular, is free of the disabilities that we have seen to plague internalism. Most obviously, reliabilism is not lacking in implications for truth; as pointed out above, it gives that consideration the highest priority. If a belief passes the reliable true belief (RTB) test, it cannot fail to be at least highly likely to be true. Second, it is not subject to the indeterminacy or arbitrariness that plagues appeals to intuition. It may, of course, be difficult or even impossible in particular cases to determine the degree of reliability of a certain belief-forming mechanism; but there is nothing arbitrary about the procedure to be employed. We simply make use of whatever resources we have for ascertaining facts in the sphere in question; there is nothing here that affords the same latitude, and temptation, to read one's theoretical prepossessions into the method.

However, the superiority I most want to stress concerns the extent of knowledge that can be recognized on each approach. We saw that internalist theories, to the extent that they do have definite implications, tend to wind up with intolerably narrow limits, with knowledge being restricted to self-evident truths, one's own conscious states, and what can be deduced from that. RTB theory, on the other hand, can recognize as knowledge whatever true beliefs are formed in a reliable way. There is no a priori guarantee of how much this takes in; but, by the same token, there are no a priori limits. It is to be decided by actual investigation in each putative area of knowledge just what reliable mechanisms are available and what knowledge they do or can produce. Thus, the field is open for perceptual knowledge about the physical environment, knowledge of the past through memory, knowledge of lawlike regularities, and so on.[53]

In addition to the ways in which externalism escapes the crippling disabilities of internalism, there are other reasons for regarding it favorably. You can think of these as reasons for reliabilism specifically; some of them will also hold for externalism generally, though I will not take time to spell that out.

A. We can think of reliabilism as generated by the marriage of source relevance and truth conducivity. I have already made some remarks by way of recommending truth conducivity. Source relevance can be supported by reflecting on the fact that if I were to possess strong reasons for a proposition but were to accept it on some disreputable basis, I could hardly be said to know it. Suppose that I actually have strong reasons for supposing that Jim is trying to get me fired, and I believe that he is, but not on the basis of those reasons (I am not really activating them from long-term memory), but just because of my paranoia. (I am given to believing this sort of thing about people even without any strong reasons for the belief.) In that case, I could hardly be said to *know* that Jim is trying to get me fired. Reflection on cases like this strongly supports the thesis that how a belief is acquired, that is, what it is based on, is crucial for its epistemic status.

B. It is plausible to suppose that what makes the difference between mere true belief and knowledge is whether it is just an accident that the belief is true. If I guess who will win the election and just happen to get it right, I can not be said to have known who would win, for it was a lucky accident that I was correct. A true belief that passes the RTB test is clearly not true by accident. If a belief was generated in a way that can be generally relied on to yield true beliefs, that is paradigmatically a nonaccidental way of getting something right.

C. Epistemologists commonly recognize a variety of factors that convert, or contribute to converting, true belief into knowledge. JTB theorists typically think of these factors as *justifiers*, but to achieve wider coverage, let us think of them as *epistemizers*, factors that make for knowledge. To focus the discussion, let us concentrate on immediate epistemizers. Popular candidates have been direct experience of the object of the belief, the mere truth of the belief for certain kinds of beliefs, the mere existence of the belief for certain kinds of belief, and the self-evidence of a proposition.[54] But what is it that makes these candidates plausible ones and leaves many other contenders (e.g., being vividly imagined or conforming to one's desires) outside the pale? An internalist will, of course, recommend a given choice by claiming that its justificatory or epistemic efficacy can be known by intuition or by reflection on one's concepts. But we have seen that these claims are, at best, terribly inflated; moreover, at best, the alleged reflection does not give us adequate insight into why it is that what justifies does so and what does not justify does not.[55] Here externalism displays its superiority by providing a simple, unified, and convincing answer to the question of what enables an epistemizer to epistemize: it is the fact that the practice of forming beliefs on the basis of the putative epistemizer is a reliable one. Surely our conviction that a belief is epistemized by one's being directly aware of what the belief is about is closely tied to our conviction that beliefs so formed are at least highly likely to be true. And the same is to be said for our conviction that any belief to the effect that one is currently in a certain conscious state is ipso facto epistemized; if one did not suppose that such beliefs are either infallible or at least very rarely mistaken, one would not be disposed to take them as epistemized just by being the kinds of beliefs they are.

VI. *Reliabilism*

Before turning to the application of externalism to the question of the knowledge of God, I will fill out the above characterization of a reliable mode of belief formation. This is all the more necessary since the viability of the notion has been widely questioned of late, and most of these attacks fail to construe the notion in its strongest form.

To say that a particular belief-forming mechanism is a reliable one is not to say that it has a favorable track record. For one thing, it may never have been used and have no track record at all, and yet it may be highly reliable in that it would compile an impressive track record if given a chance. Similarly, a thermometer might be a highly reliable instrument even if it is never used to record temperature. What the reliability of a belief-forming mechanism does amount to is the fact that it would yield a high proportion of true beliefs in a suitable run of employments. What makes a series of uses suitable? For one thing, they must be sufficiently numerous and varied. But they must also involve the kinds of situations we typically encounter. The fact that our normal, visual belief-forming mechanisms would not mostly yield truths in highly unusual environments involving laser images, clever deceptions, Cartesian demons, and the like, has no tendency to show that they are not reliable in the way relevant for epistemic evaluation. Reliability in the kinds of situations that are normal for us is what is crucial.

What proportion of truths in a suitable range of cases is needed for a degree of reliability that is sufficient for knowledge? I do not think that there is any precise answer to this question, and insofar as an answer can be given, it may well differ for different areas of knowledge. For purposes of this essay we can think of reliability as involving a high proportion of truths, say, 80 percent or so.

As is implicit in the discussion up to now, it is the reliability of particular belief-forming mechanisms, not the person, generally, that is relevant to the requirements for knowledge. Obviously, a particular person can be very good at forming some kinds of beliefs and very bad at forming others. We do not want to make it impossible for a person to have perceptual knowledge just because he is very bad at doing arithmetical calculations.

A great deal of heavy weather has been made lately over how to individuate belief-forming mechanisms and over how to determine which mechanisms are relevant to the assessment of a particular belief. With respect to my present belief that a computer screen is in front of me, what class of beliefs has to contain mostly true beliefs for this belief to pass the test: visual beliefs, visual beliefs about objects directly in front of one, beliefs about computers, beliefs formed on a Friday, and so on?[56] Puzzles such as these arise because one ignores the fact that it is belief-forming *mechanisms* that are in question here, not any old *classes* of beliefs or belief-forming processes. To know what to look at to ascertain the reliability of a particular belief, we need to determine what input-output mechanism was activated to produce that belief. Otherwise stated, we need to know what input-output function it is by virtue of which that belief was formed on the basis of the relevant input. Still otherwise stated, we need to determine what it was that the psyche was taking account of in forming that particular belief. In this example, the fact that the process took place on a Friday is highly unlikely to play any role in the production of the belief. In fact, it is highly likely that the relevant input consisted of a certain pattern of sensory data, perhaps together with certain background beliefs; anything else true of the current situation was irrelevant to the formation of that particular belief. So the question of whether this belief was reliably formed is the question of whether the activation of a function going from inputs of just that sort to a belief output of just that sort would, in a suitable spread of cases, yield mostly true beliefs.

Belief-forming mechanisms can change. Indeed, they can be acquired and lost. I did not have the tendency to go from a certain pattern of sensory data to the belief that there is a golden retriever in front of me until I had acquired the concept of a golden retriever. And if I lose my faith, I will lose the tendency to go from a belief that Jesus said that p to a belief that p. As for modification, consider the point that as we mature we move from a tendency to accept anything anyone says to a more complex testimonial mechanism that yields the belief that p not just from any belief input of the form 'S said that p'', but only from an input that also includes the belief that S satisfies certain conditions. How long-lasting must a reliable mechanism be in order that a true belief it yields thereby be qualified to count as knowledge? Again, I do not think that there is any precise answer to this, but, in any event, in this essay we will be concerned with relatively long-lasting mechanisms.

"Suppose that I am credulous enough to believe anything anyone says. On a particular occasion I accept a report of a highly reliable person. On the RTB theory I would thereby acquire knowledge since my source is reliable, but obviously I don't have knowledge in this case. Since I would accept anything anyone says, no matter how unreliable, it is just a lucky accident that I got a true belief on this occasion, and so I could not be credited with knowledge." The answer to this objection is that what is crucial for the reliability that contributes to knowledge is not the reliability of an external source but the reliability of the belief-forming mechanism that is responsible for the belief in question. The mechanism here is one that goes from any belief of the form 'S said p'' (whatever the S) to the belief that p. That mechanism is a highly unreliable one, and so beliefs formed by its activation do not count as knowledge, however reliable the S in a particular case.

VII. Reliabilism and the Possibility
of Knowledge of God

At long last we are ready to apply reliabilism to the prospects for knowledge of God. In doing so I will concentrate on cases of the sort illustrated earlier, in which a Christian believes such articles of faith as the Incarnation on the basis of assertions in the Bible or pronouncements of the church. But do not suppose that reliabilism is restricted to testimonial cases like these. Any claim to knowledge, on whatever basis, can be evaluated in terms of whether the basis on which the belief was formed is a reliable indication of the truth of the belief. I might have considered arguments in natural theology, or religious experience, or alleged miracles, as bases for one or another belief about God. I have chosen my examples in the way I have partly because they represent very common grounds for Christian belief, and partly because they seem so unpromising from the standpoint of internalist JTB theory, at least given contemporary secularist assumptions. Thus they provide an especially striking contrast between the approaches of internalism and externalism to questions of knowledge.

Before turning to the task at hand I should say a word about the status of epistemic justification on the RTB account of knowledge. I have already pointed out that I am working with a version of reliabilism that turns its back on justification and replaces it with reliability in the analysis of knowledge. That does not imply that justification is not an issue of importance in its own right, though reliabilists like Dretske and Nozick seem to think that the notion is not worth trying to reconstruct. Moreover, it might well be that knowledge typically involves justified belief, even if justification is not strictly a necessary condition. Whether this is so depends on how we construe justification. I have already argued that justification on a typical internalist construal is a commodity in very short supply. If, however, justification is equated with reliability (to put it roughly), as Goldman and Swain do, that is a completely different ball game. I do not find that identification at all plausible. I have argued elsewhere for a mixed view, according to which being justified in believing that p is a matter of *the belief's being based on an adequate ground*, with a sort of internalist constraint on grounds, though not the sort of internalist constraint we have been criticizing (the ground must be the sort of thing that is typically cognitively accessible just on reflection), and with adequacy spelled out in an externalist fashion (the ground must be a reliable basis for the belief).[57] The last clause implies a sharp difference from the internalism we have been criticizing, for it implicitly rejects any requirement that the adequacy of the ground (its justificatory efficacy) be ascertainable just on reflection. More specifically, this is an account of prima facie justification; for unqualified justification, it is also required that the subject possess no sufficient overriders, reasons for supposing the belief is false or that this particular ground is not adequate. This account opens up a much wider territory for justification than is available to pure internalists; it leaves open the possibility that, for example, perceptual beliefs about the environment are justified by being based on sense experience, even though it is not intuitively evident that sense experience is an adequate ground for such beliefs. I believe that when justification is construed in this way, it is plausible to hold that virtually all normal human knowledge involves justified belief. I believe that there are only two live possibilities for exceptions. First, there may be cases in which a true belief is based on an adequate ground, but the subject is justified in believing that the ground is not adequate; this would give us reliable true belief but not justification, because of the overrider. (If you wonder why one would believe that p on ground G if one were justified in believing that the ground is unreliable, just imagine that the subject has not actually formed the belief in unreliability for which he has a justification, or that though he has formed the belief, it is not actively operative at the moment but buried deep in memory storage.) Second, there are conceivable cases in which the input to a reliable belief-forming mechanism is of a sort that is never accessible to the subject on reflection. If the belief is true, this could be a case of reliable true belief that is not justified because the internalist constraint on the ground is not satisfied. It seems clear, however, that cases of the first sort rarely occur, and cases of the second sort perhaps never occur. When beliefs about God are formed on the basis of the Bible, or pronouncements of the church, the bases are reflectively accessible; and so if we have reliably formed beliefs here we will also have justification on my account of justification, unless, strangely enough, the believer is justified in taking the basis to be unreliable. In any event, in order to achieve maximum coverage I will confine my discussion to the question of knowledge (construed in RTB terms) and leave justification to one side. This strategy will also enable me to avoid going any further into my theory of justification.

The application of RTB theory to the knowledge claims on which we are focusing is really quite simple, but to display it with sufficient concreteness, we will need to spell out how the claims look from an RTB perspective. These are testimonial cases in which the input is simply the belief that the testifier asserts that p, and in which the output is the belief that p. I am using 'testifier' in such a way that it covers documents as well as persons. It may be that this formulation seriously oversimplifies the situation in many cases. It may be that the input is usually, or sometimes, much more complex than this, involving background beliefs about the external source or about reasons for trusting the source or about God, His nature, and his doings. However, the basic points I make would be unaffected by these complications; and so for simplicity, I will use the stripped-down account of the input-output relation just presented.

Now for the basic point to which the entire essay has been leading. Take a person who believes that God is loving because this is asserted in the Bible, or this is part of the church's official teaching. According to RTB theory, the question of whether his belief that God is loving (which we will take to be true for the sake of illustration) counts as knowledge hangs entirely (apart from possible Gettier problems, which we are leaving to one side) on whether the mechanism of belief formation responsible for the belief is a reliable one. If it is, then he knows that God is loving, whether or not he can show that the mechanism is reliable, whether or not he can show that his basis is adequate, whether or not he can provide reasons for his belief that would be convincing to any rational person who considered them carefully, and whether or not his grounds pass internalist tests. If being asserted in the Bible is a reliable indication of truth, then a person who comes to believe that p because it is asserted in the Bible thereby knows that p (assuming that p is true and that no Gettier problems are lurking in the wings). And that holds, whether or not the person has sophisticated reasons, adequate reasons, or any reasons at all for supposing the Bible to be infallible, inspired, or a reliable source of truth. A parallel point holds for ecclesiastical pronouncements. Provided the mechanism is reliable, the person gets knowledge, however inept he may be at providing reasons for this.

I am not suggesting that knowledge of the RTB sort is available only to those who lack sufficient reasons for supposing the basis of their belief to be an adequate one. The possession of such reasons will certainly not detract from a knowledge claim. It is just that it does not add to the claim either, nor is it in any way required. What those reasons provide, or contribute to, is not the lower-level knowledge that God is loving but the higher-level knowledge that one knows that God is loving. If one were to confuse knowing that p with knowing that one knows that p, or if one were to confuse being justified in believing that p with knowing, or being justified in believing, that one is justified in believing that p, then one would be led to suppose that what is required for the higher-level knowledge is also required for its lower-level correlate.[58] Freeing ourselves from that confusion, we will be able to see that one need not know, or have adequate reasons for supposing, that one's basis is reliable in order for it to *be* reliable, and that the latter is what is relevant to the question of whether the belief formed on that basis counts as knowledge. Thus the maximally unsophisticated believer who simply takes his belief from his religious community or the authoritative figures thereof, or from the Bible, without so much as wondering whether these sources are trustworthy, may still know what he believes, provided he has a firm habit of forming beliefs on the basis of these sources and the sources are reliable. But, of course, a person who forms beliefs on the same basis, but possesses reasons, adequate or inadequate, for taking the sources to be reliable, will also have knowledge for just exactly the same reasons. It is, moreover, a fine thing to have adequate reasons for supposing the bases of one's beliefs to be adequate to the task. To look into the question of which of our beliefs have adequate grounds and which do not is a task to which every rational, reflective individual is called; and, no doubt, the condition of having reflectively validated knowledge is a higher condition than the condition of merely having knowledge. Nevertheless, it is trivially true that merely having knowledge is sufficient for having knowledge. Even if the truth is not hidden from the wise and powerful and revealed *only* to babes and sucklings, it does at least extend to the latter.

I am not maintaining that the reliability of the Bible or the church is in itself sufficient for one who acquired a true belief from this source to have knowledge. Remember the previous point about knowledge, on RTB theory, hanging not on the reliability of an external source but on the reliability of the belief-forming mechanism involved. To parallel an example used there, if S believes whatever the Bible or the church says just because he is credulous enough to believe anything he reads or anything any institution proclaims, then the true beliefs he thus acquires will not count as knowledge, because the mechanism that engendered them (one that goes from any external assertion that p to belief that p) is a highly unreliable one. The mechanism must be sufficiently discriminating.[59] If, as I am supposing for the sake of illustration, the Bible is highly reliable but not all books are, and the church is highly reliable but not all institutions are, then the relevant, testimonial belief-forming mechanisms must be set up to form beliefs on the basis of reliable external sources and to reject the testimony of unreliable ones. Actually, that is overstating it. One could be much less than perfect in spotting unreliable sources and still get knowledge from reliable ones. It is difficult, or perhaps impossible, to say just how much discriminative power is required for the kind or degree of reliability required for knowledge. But it is at least clear that one who is totally undiscriminating with regard to testimony gets no knowledge that way, even though one does not have to be perfect in such discriminations to get knowledge from testimony.

Let me take this opportunity to avert a possible misunderstanding. In putting forward the Bible and the church as (possibly) adequate bases of Christian belief, I am not committing myself to any sort of fundamentalism. First, I am only discussing possibilities. Second, the use of the Bible I have in mind does not require supposing that every statement in it is true, or that it was "dictated" to its human authors by God, or that every statement is to be taken literally rather than figuratively, every narrative to be taken historically rather than parabolically or allegorically. Likewise, the appeal to the authority of the church I have in mind does not ignore the many failings of the church, even in its teaching office. What these appeals do presuppose is that God is at work in the composition and transmission of the Bible and in the life of the church in such a way as to render them, by and large, reliable sources of belief about the central concerns of the faith.

VIII. *Reliablism and the Actuality*
of Knowledge of God

So far, I have been pointing out how RTB theory leaves open possibilities for knowledge of God that are closed off by internalist· JTB theory. But my readers have undoubtedly been impatiently wondering when I am going to stop presenting mere possibilities and get down to the really interesting question of actuality. The believer will have knowledge (in the case of a true un-Gettierized belief) provided the belief is engendered by a reliable belief-forming mechanism. But how can we tell whether one or another such mechanism is reliable? Until we determine that, we will not have moved a step beyond internalist JTB theory in showing that anyone actually does have knowledge of God.

What is the approach of reliabilism to such questions? We have already touched on that. We saw that with respect to perceptual knowledge, for example, the reliabilist position is that the question of whether we do, in fact, have perceptual knowledge is, pace Gettier problems, the question of whether any of our perceptual beliefs are true, and the question of whether any of our perceptual belief-forming mechanisms are reliable. And both of these are empirical questions, questions that can be tackled only by the standard methods of empirical investigation. With respect to the latter question, we cannot expect to determine whether our standard ways of forming visual beliefs yield mostly true beliefs without looking into the ways in which they are formed and considering, in the light of what we know about human beings, their physical environment, and the interrelations thereof, what reasons there are for considering these methods of belief formation to be generally reliable. If our approach to this question is not to be maximally epistemically circular (using each perceptual belief twice: once as the tested and once as the tester), we will have to develop a general theory of perception and perceptual belief and consider what implications that theory has for the reliability of perceptual belief formation. Like any other empirical investigation, this one will necessarily make use of what we learn from sense perception in posing our questions and testing suggested answers; and so here, too, we are infected with epistemic circularity, though not so blatantly as in the simpler approach just mentioned. Thus, for reliabilism there is no escape from epistemic circularity in the assessment of our fundamental sources of belief. Since the question of whether we have perceptual knowledge depends on whether perceptual, belief-forming mechanisms are reliable, as well as on whether perceptual beliefs are true, it is ineluctably an empirical question, one that we can tackle only by relying on perceptual beliefs to do so, thereby assuming, at least in practice, that those beliefs are reliably produced.

And so it is in the realm of religion. Just as it is an empirical question whether standard, perceptual belief-forming mechanisms are reliable, so it is a theological question whether the Bible or the church is a trustworthy source of belief, and whether practices of forming beliefs on their basis are reliable. If we want to know whether, as the Christian tradition would have it, God guarantees the Bible and the church as a source for fundamental religious beliefs, what recourse is there except to what we know about God, His nature, purposes, plans, and actions? And where do we go for this knowledge? In the absence of any promising suggestions to the contrary, we have to go to the very sources of belief credentials of which are under scrutiny. Epistemic circularity is no more avoidable in this matter than it is in the assessment of basic secular sources of belief. To be sure, there have been many attempts to develop accounts of the existence and nature of God without relying on any specifically religious sources for the premises of the argument; this is the traditional enterprise of natural theology. And then there are the 'evidences of the Scriptures' and of the church, mentioned more than once in this essay. But even on the most optimistic reading of what we can learn in these ways, it falls far short of definitively settling the question of whether the specifically religious sources of belief we have been considering are reliable ones. These extrareligious sources tell us about as much about that as traditional "arguments for the existence of the external world," and other attempts to give a noncircular validation of sense perception, tell us about the reliability of sense perception, that is, very little. In neither case can we mount any impressive, nonepistemically circular arguments either for or against the reliability of the belief-forming mechanisms. We may as well face the fact that the question of the credentials of the Bible and the church is basically a theological question. That is not to say that no other sources can contribute anything. Contradictions in the Bible are certainly relevant to its degree of reliability. If it can be shown, by ordinary secular means, that the church is a Mafia operation with the primary purpose of bilking the populace, that will be highly relevant to its credibility. And perhaps the traditional evidences have at least some tendency to support the appeal to Bible and church. But after we have milked these contributions for all they are worth, we will still be short of a definitive resolution, and I do not see how we can hope to reach closure on the question without turning to theology. In like fashion, we can conclude from conflicts between perceptual beliefs that sense perception is not an infallible source of belief; but such internal investigation does not tell us how reliable it is. Generally speaking, to determine the reliability of a particular belief-forming mechanism we have to rely on what we know (or reasonably believe) about the reality with which this mechanism deals and our cognitive relations thereto. For empirical belief-forming mechanisms, this means carrying out empirical investigations, including the sophisticated version thereof known as science. And for religious belief-forming mechanisms, this means carrying out investigations into the nature and doings of God, and that means doing theology.

This conclusion will not be popular with many people, and especially with those who take themselves to have nothing to go on in carrying out theological investigations. "How," they will say, "can we investigate the nature and purposes of God and our relation thereto when we have no basis for reaching any conclusions about such matters?" That is a difficulty, the same difficulty an angel might experience in trying to settle questions about the reliability of human sense perception, assuming that the angel would lack the wherewithal for empirical investigation of the relation of sense perception to the perceived environment. But I am afraid that is the way it is. If one lacks cognitive access to a certain sphere of reality, one is doomed to ignorance thereof. If you are in that situation, you ain't never gonna know.

IX. Summary

The common supposition that we can have no knowledge of God ultimately rests on the supposition that for a knowledge claim to be correct, we must be able to determine, in a noncircular fashion, for example, just by reflection, that the belief involved is justified. But if this demand is pushed through all the way, it turns out that there is precious little we know. The kind of internalism that is behind the demand has little to recommend to it. Its externalist competitor has much more going for it as a general orientation in epistemology, and it opens up possibilities for knowledge of God that are closed to internalism. The price of this, however, is a renunciation of the aim at a noncircular demonstration of the reliability of our sources of knowledge and an abandonment of hopes for the autonomy of epistemology. This carries with it a recognition that the assessment of any alleged source of knowledge must be based on what we know about the sphere of reality allegedly known and our relations thereto. In application to religion, it implies that the epistemology of religious belief is itself a theological issue. One more nail in the coffin of the Cartesian dream.

Notes

1. Here 'faith' designates a propositional attitude, a kind of acceptance of a proposition that falls short of knowledge in its epistemic status. Different theorists give different accounts of just what propositional attitude this is. It should also be noted that 'faith' has been used for a wide variety of other religious attitudes, from trust in God to "ultimate concern." Our purposes in this essay do not require us to enter this thicket.

2. Thomas Aquinas, *Summa Theologiae* IIa, IIae, q. 1, art. 4. Aquinas holds that in the act of faith the will is moved by divine grace.

3. H. H. Price, "Some Considerations About Belief," *Proceedings of the Aristotelian Society* 35 (1934–35): 229.

4. John Locke, *Essay Concerning Human Understanding* 4, 1, ii.

5. Aquinas, *Summa Theologiae*, IIa, IIae, q. 1, art. 5.

6. For some discussion of this issue, with references to the literature, see my "Self-Warrant: A Neglected Form of Privileged Access," *American Philosophical Quarterly* 13, no. 4 (1976): 265–67. This is reprinted in my *Epistemic Justification: Essays in the Theory of Knowledge* (Ithaca, N.Y.: Cornell University Press, 1989).

7. H. A. Prichard, "Knowledge and Perception," in *Knowledge and Belief*, ed. A. P. Griffiths (London: Oxford University Press, 1967), p. 67. Prichard takes it that knowledge is coextensive with *certainty*.

8. So Aquinas: "It is impossible that one and the same thing should be believed and seen by the same person" (*Summa Theologiae* IIa, IIae, q. 1, art. 5). See also Price, "Some Considerations About Belief."

9. For an illuminating and much more extended explication of the concept, see Robert Audi, "The Concept of Believing," *The Personalist* 53, no. 1 (1972): 43–62.

10. Edmund Gettier, "Is Justified True Belief Knowledge?" *Analysis* 23 (1963): 121–23.

11. For an exploration of all this, see my "Concepts of Epistemic Justification," *The Monist* 68, no. 1 (Jan. 1985); and my "The Deontological Conception of Epistemic Justification," *Philosophical Perspectives* 2 (1988), both reprinted in my *Epistemic Justification*.

12. This conception is recommended in my "Concepts of Epistemic Justification" and also in "An Internalist Externalism," *Synthese* 74 (1988). The latter also appears in my *Epistemic Justification*.

13. Thomas Aquinas, *Summa Contra Gentiles*, 1, 6. Presumably most twentieth-century philosophers would judge that if the claims of revelation are supported as strongly as Aquinas alleges, they would thereby satisfy the justification condition for knowledge.

14. Anthony Flew, *God and Philosophy* (London: Hutchinson, 1966).

15. Anthony Flew, *The Presumption of Atheism* (London: Pemberton, 1976).

16. J. L. Mackie, *The Miracle of Theism* (Oxford: Clarendon Press, 1982).

17. Such people also typically give reasons for denying the existence of God, principally the problem of evil, thus attacking claims to satisfy the truth condition for knowledge. But since I am concentrating on the justification condition, I shall ignore that part of their work.

18. For both points, see Alvin Plantinga, "Coherentism and the Evidentialist Objection to Belief in God," in *Rationality, Religious Belief, and Moral Commitment*, ed. Robert Audi and W. J. Wainwright (Ithaca, N.Y.: Cornell University Press, 1986).

19. See, e.g., the following works by Alvin Plantinga: "Reason and Belief in God," in *Faith and Rationality*, ed. Alvin Plantinga and Nicholas Wolterstorff (Notre Dame: University of Notre Dame Press, 1983); "Is Belief in God Rational?" in *Rationality and Religious Belief*, ed. C. F. Delaney (Notre Dame: University of Notre Dame Press, 1979); "Is Belief in God Properly Basic?" *Nous* 15 (1981): 41–51.

20. See, e.g., my "Christian Experience and Christian Belief," in *Faith and Rationality*; "Religious Experience and Religious Belief," *Nous* 16 (1982): 2–12; and "Perceiving God," *Journal of Philosophy* 83 (Nov. 1986): 655–65.

21. Some would make the stronger requirement that S *know* that q. This would have the advantage of blocking Gettier problems, but I feel that it is too strong as an across-the-board requirement for mediate justification.

22. The "because" is spelled out in various ways: causality, inference, some other sort of "on the basis of" relation, and so on.

23. I will say more shortly about what this involves.

24. This requirement is less widely imposed than the others, and I find it quite indefensible. Nevertheless, it will do no harm to include it in the list for present purposes.

25. To be sure, it may be doubted that Christians hold their beliefs because of the reasons they suppose themselves to have. It has often been suggested that in all or most such cases, the beliefs would be held even in the absence of reasons, and that the reasons are performing a "rationalizing" or "cover-up" job. But this is not the sort of issue with which we are concerned in this essay. Even if (some or all) Christian beliefs genuinely rest on reasons in the way the believers suppose, the arguments against Christian knowledge with which we are concerned, those based on the alleged absence of justification, would still apply.

26. The converse does not quite hold. We could have reason to regard the Bible as reliable in theological matters without being justified in regarding it as the word of God. And, likewise, we might conceivably be justified in supposing the church to be reliable in its doctrinal pronouncements without being justified in supposing it to be guided by the Holy Spirit in those pronouncements. But typically those who do regard the Bible or the church as reliable in these matters do so for the reasons specified.

27. "This epistemology" will have to be understood here as JTB epistemology in its internalist form, as will be explained shortly.

28. See in this connection my "An Internalist Externalism," p. 278, and Laurence Bonjour, *The Structure of Empirical Knowledge* (Cambridge, Mass: Harvard University Press, 1985), pp. 7–8.

29. For a critical examination of various uses of 'internalism' and 'externalism', see my "Internalism and Externalism in Epistemology," *Philosophical Topics* 14, no. 1 (Spring 1986): 179–221, reprinted in my *Epistemic Justification*.

30. Roderick Chisholm, *Theory of Knowledge*, 3d ed. (Englewood Cliffs, N.J.: Prentice-Hall, 1989), p. 7. The passage is confusingly written; just what addition do the third and fourth sentences make to the second? Nevertheless, the import of the whole passage is clear.

31. Internalism should not be saddled with the assumption that every question about justification can be settled by reflection. It is sufficient for internalist purposes that enough such questions can be settled to enable us to make significant progress in determining what we are and are not

justified in believing, and, hence, in determining what we do and do not know.

32. Thomas Reid, *An Inquiry into the Human Mind* (Chicago: University of Chicago Press, 1970), esp. chaps. 6 and 7.

33. H. H. Price, *Perception* (London: Methuen, 1932), chap. 6.

34. Chisholm, *Theory of Knowledge.*

35. John Pollock, *Knowledge and Justification* (Princeton: Princeton University Press, 1974), p. 12.

36. Ibid., p. 21.

37. No doubt, a two-year-old child's concept of a window, a bird, or a child is quite different from the typical adult concept in many more ways than the absence of any conditions of epistemic justification. Nevertheless, once we see the possibility of forming a usable concept of a bird that involves no justification conditions, we will be rightfully encouraged to suppose that one could have a concept of a bird that is much richer than that of the child but contains no justification conditions. This would be impossible only if the various avian features that are included in the adult but not the infantile concept are necessarily tied to justification conditions. And no one has provided any reason for supposing this to be the case.

38. Richard Foley, *The Theory of Epistemic Rationality* (Cambridge, Mass: Harvard University Press, 1987).

39. Ibid., p. 66.

40. Reid, *Inquiry Into the Human Mind*, pp. 81–82.

41. Ibid., p. 207.

42. For more on this see my "Yes, Virginia, There Is a Real World," *Proceedings and Addresses of the American Philosophical Association* 52, no. 6 (August 1979).

43. Proponents of the approaches we have been discussing, almost without exception, acknowledge that justification, as they are treating it, has no logical connection with truth. Thus, Chisholm: "According to this traditional conception of 'internal' epistemic justification, there is no *logical* connection between epistemic justification and truth" (Chisholm, *Theory of Knowledge*, p. 7). See also Foley, *Theory of Epistemic Rationality*, chap. 3. This denial of truth conducivity is reflected in the contention that in a "demon world" in which our perceptions are radically unreliable, or even invariably false, our perceptual beliefs would be justified in just the same way as they are in our world (even assuming that in

the actual world perception is generally reliable). See Foley, *Theory of Epistemic Rationality*, pp. 158–59.

44. A. I. Goldman, "What is Justified Belief?" in *Justification and Knowledge*, ed. G. S. Pappas (Dordrecht: Reidel, 1979); A. I. Goldman, *Epistemology and Cognition* (Cambridge, Mass: Harvard University Press, 1986); Marshall Swain, *Reasons and Knowledge* (Ithaca, N.Y.: Cornell University Press, 1981).

45. See, e.g., Fred Dretske, *Knowledge and the Flow of Information* (Cambridge, Mass: MIT Press, 1981); Robert Nozick, *Philosophical Explanations* (Cambridge, Mass: Harvard University Press, 1981), chap. 3.

46. I will explain, below, how justification, as I conceive it, fits into knowledge.

47. I will spell out this notion in a bit more detail, below, though I will not be able to give a full treatment.

48. Here are some other forms of externalism. 1. The *causal* theory: Some appropriate causal relation of the belief to its object is what converts true belief into knowledge. 2. The *counterfactual* theory: True belief is knowledge provided that there would not be that belief unless it were true. 3. The *proper functioning* theory: Knowledge is true belief engendered by cognitive faculties functioning properly.

49. The reader will remember that we formulated a principle of mediate justification for the internalist in "source relevant" terms. Condition 3 contains the requirement that the belief is based on the reason in question.

50. Since a belief may change its epistemic status after being acquired (if, e.g., the subject comes into possession of additional evidence), it is an oversimplification to say that the epistemic status of a belief depends on how it was produced initially. A more adequate formulation would be in terms of what supports the belief, what is responsible for its existence, either at the moment of acquisition or at various further stages of its career. However, in this brief treatment we will avail ourselves of the oversimplification and speak merely in terms of how the belief was originally acquired.

51. If the term 'naturalism' is to be used here, we shall have to recognize, as will be brought out in the final section, that, as with G. E. Moore's "naturalism" in meta-epistemology, supernaturalism is a form of naturalism.

52. In my "Epistemic Circularity," in *Epistemic Justification*, I seek to show that epistemic circularity in an argument does not prevent us from

using that argument to show that a belief or beliefs that meet certain conditions are justified or reliably formed.

53. There is also the point that RTB does not suffer from the blind spot regarding intuition and reflection we have seen to plague internalism. Externalism can investigate the reliability of these mechanisms in basically the same way it investigates any others. However, this is not a very impressive point, given that what keeps internalism from validating intuition is epistemic circularity, and given that, as we have just seen, externalism embraces epistemic circularity in its investigations into knowledge, or at least has learned to live with it.

54. See my "Self-Warrant" for a comparative discussion of such candidates.

55. See John Pollock, *Contemporary Theories of Knowledge* (Totowa, N.J.: Rowman and Littlefield, 1986), pp. 94–96, for a similar complaint against forms of internalism other than his own.

56. See, e.g., Richard Feldman, "Reliability and Justification," *The Monist* 68, no. 2 (April 1985).

57. See my "An Internalist Externalism."

58. See my "Level Confusions in Epistemology," *Midwest Studies in Philosophy* 5 (1980), reprinted in my *Epistemic Justification*.

59. This point is well brought out in A. I. Goldman, "Discrimination and Perceptual Knowledge," *Journal of Philosophy* 73 (1976): 771–91.

2

RATIONALITY AND

RELIGIOUS COMMITMENT

Philosophical discussions of faith and reason must avoid at least two quite natural mistakes. One mistake is to draw a naive contrast that puts faith and reason on opposite sides in human life. People sometimes express this polarity when they say, of a position for which they think there is no significant evidence, that it must simply be believed "on faith." The second mistake—or so I shall argue—is the attempt to reconcile faith and reason by assimilating faith, or at least any kind of faith regarded as consonant with reason, to rational belief. It is this second mistake that I especially want to examine. The issue is important for the overall topic of the rationality of religious commitment. For if faith, or even one major kind of faith, *is* a species of belief, then the rationality of religious faith must be decided largely on the basis of an account of rational belief. It may well be, of course, that the relevant kinds of religious belief are rational and can be shown to be so. Part of this essay assesses the prospects for this. But it also explores the possibility that a religious commitment, with faith as its central element, can be rational even if theistic beliefs, particularly the kind philosophers have defended by argument, should turn out not to be. My strategy is both to emphasize some respects in which faith is a distinct kind of attitude and, in that light, to redirect some of the discussion of the rationality of religious commitment toward giving faith, as distinct from belief, a larger role.

In approaching the rationality of religious faith, religious belief, or indeed any cognitive religious attitude, we should avoid being narrow in three ways that are common in philosophical literature. First, philosophers and others often underestimate the extent to which their conception of the issues is shaped by skepticism. Second, religious commitment, even when taken to be equivalent to faith, is often considered mainly cognitive, or at least more cognitive than it is.[1] Third, even when discussions of religious commitment are restricted to the cognitive domain, they tend to be preoccupied with the possibility of knowledge of God, or at least with the possibility that theistic beliefs are justified in a strong sense, a sense in which, if they are true, they constitute knowledge. I am interested in both of these possibilities, and particularly in *evidentialism:* the view that neither theistic knowledge, nor even justified theistic belief, is possible except on the basis of evidence. But I also want to consider noncognitive religious commitments. Indeed, they must be addressed if we are to achieve an adequate understanding of the general topic of faith and reason.

My aim, then, is to provide a partial theory of the overall rationality of religious commitment, taking account of both cognitive and noncognitive dimensions and, within the cognitive field, distinguishing between doxastic and fiduciary attitudes. Part I lays the groundwork: noting—and forswearing—certain skeptical influences on the treatment of the rationality issue, sorting out several dimensions of the issue, and arguing for the possibility of construing it largely in terms of rationality as opposed to justification and of a concept of religious faith not reducible to some notion of religious belief. Part II explores the prospects for dealing with the rationality issue by arguing for the nonevidential justification of certain theistic beliefs. And Part III outlines a different, more modest approach that centers on the notion of faith characterized in Part I.

I. *Toward a Redirection*
of the Reconciliation
of Faith and Reason

Skeptical Influences on Epistemological Thinking

Skepticism has profoundly affected philosophical thinking about knowledge, justification, and indeed rationality in general. It influences those who reject it as well as those who accept some form of it or suspend judgment on it. Let me mention just two of its major effects.

First, skepticism inclines most who think about knowledge, justification, and related cognitive concepts to adopt, even if implicitly or unconsciously, extremely high standards of adequacy; for instance, to suppose that knowledge requires certainty and that justified belief requires powerful or even conclusive evidence. This epistemic rigorism is a natural response to skeptics because they so vividly point out a multitude of ways in which we can be mistaken. Realizing that we cannot have knowledge of a falsehood, and generally believing that we are not justified unless we have grounds that at least tend to preclude mistake, we are tempted to think that knowledge requires conclusive evidence and justified belief something close to that.[2]

Second—and this point has only recently been shown in detail —when, in the shadow of skepticism, we theorize about knowledge, justification, and related cognitive notions, we tend to believe that we *have* knowledge or justification only if we also believe that our grounds for it, such as our visual experiences, enable us to *show* that we have it. Skeptics often make us feel that if we truly stand on solid ground, then we can show its solidity.[3] This is one reason why there has been such a strong tendency to regard knowledge of the external world as based on prior, more secure knowledge of sense-data, conceived as immediate and unmistakable contents of sensory consciousness. Think of Descartes: My beliefs about the colors and shapes in my visual consciousness (or certain of these beliefs) are infallible; and given the goodness and power of God, if I am sufficiently careful not to form a belief about the external world until I have, before my mind, at least one clear and distinct proposition that deductively grounds that belief, then I shall not err in holding it. Thus, not only can I have knowledge of the external world; by appeal to God's (self-evident) goodness and power, I can also show that I do. I need only note that my premises are self-evidently infallible and self-evidently entail my conclusions.

As this example suggests, preoccupation with the skeptic does more than incline us to seek ultimate premises for which we have conclusive grounds. It also inclines us to suppose that only what is *deducible* from such premises can be known, or justifiedly believed, on the basis of them. After all, if the connection between premises and conclusion is only inductive—thus in some sense probabilistic—one can start with true premises and still draw a false conclusion. Hume saw this; and, having neither a purely rational way, nor a theological route, to guarantee that inductive inferences are truth-preserving, he concluded that they do not yield knowledge of their conclusions, and hence that we do not even know that the sun will rise tomorrow.[4]

I cannot discuss skepticism in detail here; but the view I shall presuppose is that it can be *rebutted,* even if not *refuted.* That is, the case for it can be shown to be unsound, even if the view itself cannot be shown to be mistaken, say by establishing that we *do* have knowledge of the external world. Moreover, even if we cannot rebut first-order skepticism—roughly, skepticism regarding our beliefs concerning ourselves or the world—we have excellent grounds for rejecting an associated second-order view about the status of our first-order beliefs: namely, the idea that if we cannot show that we know or justifiedly believe that we have knowledge or justified beliefs about ourselves or the world, then we *lack* that knowledge or justified belief.[5] This second-order view is born of confusion. It conflates what is required to *have* such first-order knowledge or justification with what it takes to *show* that we do.

A conflation of orders is understandable when we discuss knowledge and justification in the shadow of the skeptical view that we lack them. Still, the question of what knowledge and justification *are* is different from, and indeed prior to, the question whether we have them. We must answer the first in its own terms, without the distorting burden of tacitly preparing ourselves to meet the skeptical charge that the notions we characterize are empty. The same holds for rationality, which is a close cousin of justification. Rationality (for reasons I shall shortly suggest) is the broader and less stringent notion, but it is equally normative and structurally parallel.[6]

These points are important background for the issue of the rationality of religious commitment. Above all, they can help us to avoid using unreasonably high standards of rationality or confusing first- and second-order questions. But they are also useful in another way. They help us to understand the analogy between justification of religious beliefs and other kinds of justification, notably perceptual and scientific justification. The perceptual cases offer paradigms of knowledge and justification; the scientific domain contains models of rational belief formation. Moreover, science is extremely influential in current thinking about all of these notions, and it is essential that we neither exaggerate nor underrate its capacity to provide knowledge and justification.[7] If we err in either direction, we may thereby adopt a false model for understanding these notions in the religious domain, where they are even more controversial and even harder to explicate.[8]

Dimensions of Rationality
in Religious Commitment

Against this background, I want to distinguish various dimensions of religious commitment to which questions of rationality apply. I begin with general points about the *kinds* of response one can make to issues about the rationality of religious commitment as expressed in religious belief. I then consider justification in the cognitive domain and proceed to other domains in which religious commitment occurs.

To anyone concerned with the rationality of religious commitment, there are at least three major dimensions of the issue as it arises for religious belief, as distinct from conduct and emotion. The first is *ontological:* It concerns what kind of purported reality we are talking about when we speak of God (or of certain other religiously significant beings). The traditional view, at least as philosophers have tended to interpret it, is notoriously strong: God is omniscient, omnipotent, and omnibenevolent. But, like process philosophers of religion, one might reduce the strength of theistic claims by qualifying this list, say in denying that omnipotence is essential to God.[9] The second dimension—the *semantic*—is closely related to the first. The most notable contrast here is between cognitivism and noncognitivism: The former maintains, and the latter denies, that sentences about God express propositions, hence truths or falsehoods as opposed to, say, spiritual attitudes or symbolic pictures.[10] Third, there is a wide range of *epistemic* dimensions. These concern both the cognitive—roughly, the proposition-expressive—attitude we take as central and the kinds of grounds appropriate to that attitude as held by a rational person. We can make knowledge of God our main focus, or concentrate on justified theistic belief, or simply on rational theistic belief; or indeed we may choose an attitude like faith or hope and argue that the standards of rationality appropriate to it are quite different from those that govern belief.[11]

Religious commitment also has a particularly important noncognitive (or at least not purely cognitive) dimension: the *behavioral*. Religions differ in the conduct to which they commit or incline their adherents; and if we are concerned with the *overall* rationality of religious commitment, it matters greatly whether this commitment affects the whole of one's life, or both its moral and its narrowly religious dimensions, or only the latter. Other things being equal, the wider and deeper the overall religious commitment, the more is needed, in the way of evidence or grounds or other support, to render it rational. Behavior as well as cognition is important, then, as are attitudes, emotions, and other elements in human life that are shaped by religious commitments.

The ontological dimension of religious commitment, then, concerns *what* we hold; the semantic dimension, the *kind of mean-*

ing—say, literal or figurative—appropriate to what we hold; the epistemic dimension, the *kind of attitude* with which we hold it and the grounds appropriate to that attitude; and the behavioral dimension, the *range of conduct* incumbent on us, or likely from us, by virtue of what we hold. Skepticism tends to push those concerned with the rationality of their religion toward weaker commitments in all four domains. One of my aims is to show how one may resist skepticism without resorting to any of the strong measures it often makes attractive: *ontological attenuation* of the concept of God, say into an impersonal force; *noncognitivist transformation* of religious language into expressive discourse without truth value; *dogmatism* about the epistemic status of religious belief, say by flatly insisting that religious truths are known in a way that makes inquiry into grounds irrelevant; and *detachment of religious conduct* from the associated theistic beliefs, either by justifying it in a completely independent way or by maintaining that it stands in need of no justification.

I begin with the cognitive aspects of religious commitment, which, among the four, have certainly received the most philosophical attention. In this domain there is not only the possibility of knowledge or justified belief regarding God, but of faith and hope. I especially want to clarify the notion of faith—or at least one notion of faith—and to explore the rationality of religious cognitive commitment in relation to faith conceived as an attitude significantly different from belief.

Faith and Belief.   The term 'faith' is used quite variously, and this essay makes no attempt to account for all of the associated concepts. To cite a few varieties, there is faith regarding a particular outcome, such as a recovery from a disease; there are attitudes of faith concerning large segments of human life, such as interracial relations; there is a person's faith, conceived as a religious affiliation; and there is the overall characteristic, being a person of faith, say of deep religious faith. My concern is not to sort out or unify all of these cases but to single out one important kind of faith whose importance has been largely unnoticed or widely underestimated, and to show how it bears on the rationality of religious commitment. Other kinds of faith will be considered for comparison, but our purposes do not require that any concept of faith be given a detailed analysis.

Almost any conception of faith will admit of a distinction between two related kinds. One is faith *in*—which I shall call *attitudinal faith*. It may be illustrated by the faith of one friend in another, as well as by faith in God. Since this kind of faith is toward a person or a particular nonpropositional entity such as an institution, it might also be called *objectual faith*. The second kind is faith *that*—*propositional faith*. The latter is commonly exemplified by faith that a person will succeed in something which is in some way difficult. Whether in secular or religious cases, propositional faith does not require an attitude of flat-out belief toward its (propositional) object. The meaning of 'flat-out belief' can best be brought out by contrasting such belief with a heterogeneous group of attitudes which may be conflated with it. What I have in mind is roughly this: simply and unqualifiedly believing the relevant proposition (p), as opposed to such things as (1) believing p to be probable, (2) believing it to be certain, (3) half believing it, (4) accepting it, in the sense of taking it as true,[12] (5) being disposed to believe it, and (6) "implicitly believing" it. Implicit belief occurs when, for example, one believes p conditionally, as where one believes that *if q, then p*, takes the condition, q, to be satisfied, yet does not "explicitly" believe p, say because one has never put the two separate beliefs together. For most of what we believe, it may well be true that we believe it flat-out. I believe that cars are going by, that the population of Lincoln is over 175,000, that the season has been dry. The significance of 'flat-out' is almost entirely in what it precludes, such as half believing or merely believing to be fairly likely; and in most belief ascriptions we may (as I will) omit the term with little risk of misunderstanding. By way of further clarification, let us pursue the contrasts just drawn between unqualified belief and related notions.

Consider first (1) a person's believing that p is probable. Some people seem to treat this as a case of believing, and we may do so; but it is not equivalent to believing *that p,* which is the proposition in question. (2) Believing that *p* is certain is not equivalent to (any kind of) believing that *p* either, though it may entail believing that *p,* at least in a rational person. (3) Half believing that *p* may entail "going along with" *p* up to a certain point but implies a lack of the overall *cognitive commitment,* as we might call it, characteristic of unqualifiedly believing. (4) Accepting *p*—when this is not just a matter of believing it, as on many uses of 'accept'— can be a matter of something like forming an intention to use it as a basis of inference, or taking it as a basis for conduct. Neither kind of acceptance entails believing that *p.* As for (5) being disposed to believe *p,* for instance that this essay is printed in black ink, such a disposition is a readiness to *come* to believe *p* and is easily confused with actually believing it dispositionally rather than occurrently; but being disposed to believe is importantly different from dispositionally believing.[13] (6) Finally, since a person can fail to put two and two together, believing that *p* is not entailed even by "implicit belief" of it, for instance believing both that *q* and that if *q* then *p.*

It is true that faith that, say, God loves us implies a disposition to believe that God loves us, just as faith that a friend will recover from an illness implies a disposition to believe *that* proposition. Moreover, these dispositions tend to be realized by perceptions of certain positive signs, such as a pervasive sense of God's protecting one, or the discovery of the friend's improvement. But even readily realized dispositions to believe are not, and do not entail, beliefs; and this is one among other reasons why propositional faith does not entail having the corresponding belief. Indeed, at least in nonreligious contexts the closer one comes to having that belief, the less natural it is to speak of faith rather than simply belief. It is doubtless possible to have faith that something is so when one also believes it is, but such faith does not entail belief. It may be *nondoxastic.*[14]

One reason why (propositional) faith may seem to imply belief is that it is apparently incompatible with *dis*belief. If I believe that not-p, surely I cannot have faith that p, just as I cannot (at least normally) believe both that p and that not-p.[15] I *can* have such faith compatibly with an absence of any feeling of certitude regarding p, and even with a belief that p is not highly probable. But if I disbelieve p, I do not have faith that it is so. Moreover, while I need not (and perhaps cannot) have a sense of certitude regarding the proposition, there are limits to how much doubt I can feel toward it. When the strength of doubt that p is true reaches a certain point, hope, but not faith, will likely be my attitude. Hope that p may be so desperate as to coexist with as much doubt as is possible consistently with not reaching certainty that not-p. Faith may alternate with such doubt, but it cannot coexist with any doubt sufficient to undermine a basically positive overall outlook.

To be sure, there are uses of 'faith' for which the contrast with belief is inappropriate. Unqualified belief that God loves us may be an article of one's *religious faith* in the most common sense of that phrase—the *credal sense*—in which one can lay out one's religious faith by carefully formulating its content. But if one's cognitive attitude is belief that God loves us, then (in everyday as opposed to theological and other special contexts) it is misleading to call it faith *that* he does. The point is more easily grasped in a context in which no major philosophical issue is at stake: If, from previous experience (or indeed for whatever reason), I unqualifiedly believe that Felicia will meet a certain challenge, I will tend not to express my attitude by saying I have faith that she will; for saying this would at least normally imply that I do not actually believe it. Or, consider a case in which we are worrying about whether a student with a mixed record will be able to complete a dissertation. If I have faith that the student will do the job, then, while I cannot merely have a hope that the student will, must I believe it? And if, despite the mixed record, I urge my colleagues to have faith, must I be urging belief, or suggesting that the evidence warrants belief? The cognitive attitude I am urging must be strong enough to undergird positive behavior, such as giving the student another year of support; but the attitude does not seem to imply belief that the dissertation will be completed.

Religious faith is so often identified with a set of doctrines taken to be believed by people *of* that faith that it is easy to overlook the cases in which faith that *p* does not embody the corresponding belief, that is, that *p*. Not every such (propositional) *attitude* of faith is part of a religious faith in the *doctrinal* sense; nor is every such attitude of faith held in the way often thought appropriate to the articles of faith that largely constitute religious doctrines. One may grow into faith that something is so without its ever being presented as correct doctrine, or even avowed in any way in one's presence.

The distinction I am drawing between belief and propositional faith can be brought out further by noting three related contrasts. First, whereas if one believes that *p*, even if weakly and tentatively, and *p* then turns out to be false, one has thereby been shown *mistaken* (and to be wrong about *p*). This does not always hold for faith that *p*: One's faith might be shown to be *misplaced*, and it would be *disappointed*; but one might have had a kind or degree of doubt regarding *p*, or fear that not-*p*, rather different from the kind or degree of these consistent with belief. If the student never does the dissertation, then perhaps I should not have had the faith I did have, but I need not be shown to be mistaken by this failure, as is my optimistic colleague who simply believed the student would do it. Particularly if my faith was justified, I was not mistaken in holding it, and it, as opposed to its propositional object, is not shown to be mistaken. A related contrast is this: Other things being equal, for believing that *p* as opposed to having faith that *p*, there is more tendency to be surprised upon discovering not-*p* to be the case. This contrast in turn goes well with a third: Granting that strong faith that *p* tends to preclude doubt that *p*, and granting, too, that weak belief that *p* is compatible with a significant degree of such doubt, faith that *p*, as compared with belief that *p*, is compatible with a higher *degree* of doubt that *p*. Taken together, these contrasts surely support the view that propositional faith neither reduces to belief nor even entails it.

This is not in the least to imply that belief and propositional faith are utterly different kinds of attitudes. Far from it: Both are cognitive; both admit of rationality; both influence behavior; and both vary in many of the same dimensions, such as strength and centrality to the person's outlook on the world. Beyond that, I grant that in some cases change in a single dimension, notably that of confidence regarding the proposition in question, can cause faith that does not embody belief to evolve into faith that does. Is the sort of propositional faith I am talking about, then, a kind of tentative belief? I think not. In one sense, 'tentative belief' designates (roughly) belief which, whether strong or weak, is held with a self-conscious openness to reviewing the relevant grounds. This is certainly not what propositional faith is, though it is compatible with such an attitude. In the other relevant sense, 'tentative belief' designates belief that is simply tentatively *held*, quite apart from whether there is the kind of self-conscious (often second-order) attitude just described. But surely propositional faith need not be held in this way, even if belief that *p* is not implied by it. The steadfastness of the attitude is not so simply related to its cognitive strength measured on a spectrum that ranges from inkling at one end to absolute confidence at the other. Nondoxastic propositional faith can be steadfast; weak belief— roughly the kind closer to inkling than to certitude—though not steadfast, need not be tentative. I suggest, then, that the similarities between nondoxastic propositional faith as described above and the corresponding beliefs, though significant, are consistent with treating such faith as distinctive in the ways I suggest; and even if the only major difference between propositional faith that does, and propositional faith that does not, embody belief, should be one of confidence, that would be significant. It would at least affect the standards of rationality and justification appropriate to the faith. For other things being equal, the greater the confidence embodied in a cognitive attitude toward a proposition, the more is required for the rationality or justification of that attitude.

It might seem that even if propositional faith is not reducible to a kind of belief, it is reducible to a complex of beliefs and attitudes, for example to some degree of belief that p and a positive attitude toward p's being the case. It is true that faith implies some degree of positive attitude toward the state of affairs in question; but adding such an attitude to belief is still not sufficient for propositional faith. We do not, for example, have faith that something will occur simply because we believe that it will and we have a positive attitude toward its occurrence. Far from salvaging a reductionist strategy of analyzing faith in terms of belief, this move shows that in addition to finding an appropriate belief component, the reductionist would have to show this belief to imply an appropriate attitude. I doubt that either of these conditions can be met. I leave open whether propositional faith (of any kind) is simply unanalyzable; my concern here is mainly to argue that if it is, belief need not be a constituent in the analysis.

Attitudinal Faith.   When we come to attitudinal faith, we find certain differences from its propositional counterpart. Let us first consider theological contexts, though the distinction between propositional and attitudinal faith is also important in other domains. A correct attribution of faith in God seems to *presuppose* God's existence, in that—apart from uses of the term in scare quotes, as in ironic ascriptions of faith—we cannot have faith in a nonexistent being. But this ontological presupposition can be true even when the person of faith holds associated cognitive attitudes as modest as presuming the relevant truths, as where someone with faith in a friend acts on the presumption that the friend will come through in a relevant way, such as by keeping a promise. A presumption of this kind does not require holding the proposition in the unqualified way appropriate to flatly believing it. Perhaps even *strong* faith *in* God is compatible with a cognitive theistic presupposition as modest as faith that, say, God is sovereign, where this propositional faith is of a kind incompatible both with doubting that tenet and with being sure of it in the way often appropriate to flat-out belief. Again, a nonreligious analogy may help: If I have a beneficent uncle who has disappeared and, without my knowledge, lives incognito, I might have faith in him (as good person) by virtue of a positive attitude grounded in my receiving anonymous gifts from him that I doubt would come from anyone else; yet, being quite uncertain whether this uncle is still living, I have propositional faith, and not a belief, that he is alive. It is in him that I believe because he is the existing object (and indeed source) of my attitude; yet the cognitive fiduciary elements in my attitudinal faith are not beliefs: Their propositional objects, though held in faith, are neither believed nor disbelieved.

Hope. A related phenomenon is religious hope, say the hope that this is a world in which God is sovereign and redemption is forthcoming. Religious hope is of course compatible with faith in God, and such hope typically implies that faith. But (as noted earlier) hope is compatible with a high degree of doubt, and religious hope is consistent with, though it does not require, believing that what is hoped for is not likely. In part for these reasons, it is arguable that someone who had only hope toward religiously significant propositions, and not something stronger in the way propositional faith is, could not meet the conditions for believing in God, as opposed to, say, hoping that God exists. In any case, religious hope is like the kind of propositional faith I have been describing in at least one important respect: It does not imply belief that God exists.

When one notes that hope, unlike propositional faith, does not entail the same kind of positive attitude toward the relevant object, in this case the event or state of affairs hoped for, it may seem that even passionate religious hope may be too thin to serve as the foundation of a cognitive outlook appropriate to religious commitment. But a case can surely be made that if such hope is, in a certain way, basic in one's life, it might be a sufficient foundation. I shall not argue for this, but the case I make for the suitability of faith as a foundation might also be largely applicable to hope. Other things being equal, hope would provide a weaker and perhaps religiously less significant foundation, but it might still provide something of genuine religious significance.[16]

Rationality, Justification, and External Versus
Internal Reconciliations of Faith and Reason

Once we distinguish between religious belief and other religious attitudes, we can see an important point about their rationality: The criteria for rational faith and rational hope, construed as cognitive attitudes (since they have truth-valued propositional objects),[17] are less stringent than those for rational belief. Again, it is best to start with nonreligious cases. I can have rational faith, and certainly a rational hope, that a friend will overcome a tendency to denigrate others, even though I know that I have little evidence on the matter. I might even realize that my evidence makes the friend's reforming at best an even bet; but I need not have any probability belief at all about this outcome. Moreover, although rational faith that something is so requires much stronger grounds than rational belief that it is *possible*, the former is achievable on the basis of considerably weaker grounds than those needed for rational belief that it *is* the case. To be sure, *rational* faith requires that one not have good reason for believing an obviously incompatible proposition—unless the counterreason is ultimately defeated.[18] But rational faith still implies a lesser degree of positive grounding than does rational belief. Rational faith is epistemically less at risk than rational belief. The former can withstand counterevidence better than the latter, other things being equal. The rationality of faith does, however, imply a disposition to deal in some rational way with what one takes to be counterevidence, though one need not believe that there is such evidence. This disposition is one of the sources of a sense of the possibility of error and is often accompanied by that sense. That sense in turn partly explains why having faith is sometimes associated with taking a risk.

A related point concerns the difference between justification and rationality. Surely the grounding required for rational faith—as opposed to irrational faith—is weaker than that required for justified—as opposed to unjustified—faith. The same holds for rational as opposed to justified belief. Skeptical influences tend to make us look to very high epistemic standards and assimilate rationality to justification; for we become preoccupied not only with the task of defending ourselves—a job whose success is widely felt to require justification of a strong kind—but also with trying to provide grounds that would bring a neutral or even hostile party over to our side. There are, however, crucial differences between rationality and justification. For one thing, rationality is the more global notion. While everything that admits of justification also admits of rationality, the converse does not hold. It is particularly important that persons may be rational but not—except in relation to individual elements such as actions—justified. Indeed, it is arguable that when specific elements like actions or beliefs are rational, it is above all because they are appropriate to a rational person.

This brings us to a second point: Very roughly, rational faith and rational beliefs are grounded in a way appropriate to a rational person's holding them, whereas justified beliefs must rest on specific grounds of the kind such that, when cognitions based on those grounds are true, they tend to constitute knowledge,[19] and justified propositional faith, though it does not necessarily meet this condition, perhaps tends to be closer to meeting it than faith that is simply rational. The difference in breadth, however, is not the only one. Rationality is more a matter of minimal permissibility, justification more a matter of a kind of ground specifically connected with what we tend to conceive as the basic truth-conducive sources, above all perception, introspection, memorial impressions, and conceptual reflection.

The suggested contrast between rationality and justification goes with a distinction between what we might call *internal* and *external* reconciliations of faith and reason: The former shows their compatibility in the life of a religious person, or a kind or range of kinds of religious person; the latter shows that the rational grounds for faith are sufficient to render a rational, theistically neutral person—one to whom these grounds are at least initially external—justified in adopting a theistic position. (It might, to be sure, also allow the person to be justified, or at least not unjustified, in suspending judgment on it.) The former stresses rationality more than justification, the latter justification more than rationality. As compared with justification, rationality is more readily achieved by a cognitive outlook satisfactory by one's own lights, though some intersubjective standards, such as consistency, are clearly relevant. Justification is more a matter of meeting a minimal intersubjective standard, including an appropriate cognitive grounding in the basic, apparently truth-conducive sources. If we stress faith as a—or perhaps the—central cognitive attitude in religion, and rationality rather than justification as the focus of our concern to reconcile reason and religion, the prospects for reconciliation are surely improved.

This is a good place to reiterate that religious commitment of a full-blooded kind is never *just* cognitive, but also behavioral and attitudinal. Consider its behavioral side. There are at least three important dimensions: One is spiritual, another moral, yet another aesthetic. The paradigm of religious behavior is worship, in the broad sense that includes nonverbal forms of praise or homage. But ceremonies, devotions, and other, less structured practices are also among the many things appropriate to behavior that manifests religious commitment. In addition, religious commitment normally has moral implications, and when moral behavior is in part motivated by, or at least significantly influenced by, religious commitments favoring behavior of that kind, that behavior itself counts as a manifestation of religious commitment. Similar points apply to the aesthetic, for instance to building cathedrals as an expression of religious devotion, though here the relation to religious commitment may be less direct, depending largely on whether the aesthetic activity is considered scripturally prescribed or is otherwise religiously commanded. Still, artistic creation in general may often be conceived as a form of worship or at least of reverent celebration of God.

Where conduct is implied by religious commitment, it may receive rational support from its religious source. Whether it actually does receive this support depends mainly on two factors: on whether there is, or at least the agent has adequate reason to believe there is, rational grounding for the source, say for the moral sovereignty of God, and on whether the agent has adequate reason to believe that the conduct is supported by the source, for instance evidence that a certain moral stance is indeed God's will. I see no reason to doubt that significant rational support can thus accrue to various kinds of conduct. But it is essential to realize that the same conduct may receive support from independent sources, and much religiously prescribed moral conduct is in precisely this category.

Framework for Conceiving the Rationality of Cognitive Religious Commitment

I want to begin the next stage of this exploration of the rationality of religious commitment with some broad, epistemological remarks. The dominant epistemological perspective in Western Philosophy has been foundationalist: We find this outlook in Plato and Aristotle, in Aquinas, in Descartes, and in most later rationalists and empiricists. The perspective has been qualified and much refined in this century, particularly in the past two decades. I believe that in some form—one which takes proper account of the epistemic role of coherence—it is a sound basis for discussing not only knowledge, but also justification and rationality.[20] From a foundationalist point of view, determining whether a belief is justified requires considering it as a candidate either for foundational status—and hence as noninferentially, even if defeasibly, justified—or for derivative justification—and hence as justified inferentially on the basis of one or more prior beliefs expressing evidence for it. The same holds for rationality, but I shall first focus on justification and knowledge in order to make connections with some recent philosophical literature.

Foundationalism as just characterized is neutral regarding skepticism; and, conceptually as well as historically, it provides a good framework for understanding skepticism. Both patterns just specified, the foundational and the inferential, indicate possible antiskeptical approaches, though each can also be pursued independently of skepticism, for instance as a way to gain understanding of God or of aspects of the religious life.[21] The attempt to establish God's existence by argument fits the inferential pattern: God's existence, as well as certain truths about God, are taken to be knowable, or at least justifiedly believable, on the basis of prior premises—on some views even self-evident premises. By contrast, the thesis that God, or at least certain theistic propositions, can be directly and noninferentially known in experience represents the noninferential pattern. On this view, both knowledge of God and certain justified beliefs about God, are grounded in experience and not in *prior* beliefs of evidence propositions— beliefs which themselves might need justification. This *experientialist tradition*, as I shall call it, has both mystical and nonmystical branches. The *evidentialist tradition*, by contrast, contends that if there is knowledge or justified belief about God, it is based on prior evidence, such as good arguments. Experientialism takes God to be, as it were, among the premises, or at least to be an object of knowledge not itself dependent on prior premises. Evidentialism regards knowledge and justified belief about God as accessible only inferentially, hence only through premises knowable or justifiedly believable on the basis of propositions that do not epistemically presuppose God's existence.

My main concern in this section and the next is with cognitive commitment, and above all with the issue of evidentialism versus experientialism. I am not concerned with arguments for God's existence (a topic on which there is a vast literature). I believe, however, that neither any sound epistemological framework, nor anything in the *concept* of a spiritual reality, or of God in particular, establishes that knowledge (or justified belief) that God exists cannot be established by argument, even if not by any single, knockdown argument. In addition to the possibility of mutually supporting arguments, there is a possibility of justification derived from argument taken together with justification grounded experientially. Both possibilities should be noted for our purposes, but need not be discussed.[22]

What about the possibility—far less often discussed than arguments for God's existence—of *direct* knowledge—noninferential and hence nonevidential knowledge—of God? Contrary to widespread belief, general epistemological considerations do not rule out such knowledge. Indeed, suppose there can be what I call *natural knowledge*, as in the case of direct and instantly produced knowledge, by an idiot savant, of arithmetical results ordinarily knowable only through lengthy calculation. If such natural knowledge is possible, there is some reason to think that knowledge can come from a built-in capacity which might in principle yield direct knowledge of God. To be sure, at least for those who think that knowledge must have a partly biological basis in the brain, there may be less mystery about how a calculational mechanism could be built into the brain than about how knowledge of an external, spiritual reality could be received or sustained by the brain as we know it. Still, an omnipotent God could create such direct knowledge. If there can be such knowledge, then one form of evidentialism is mistaken, namely, *evidentialism about knowledge*, the view that knowledge of God is impossible except on the basis of adequate evidence. The task of the next two sections will be to explore the case against evidentialism and for direct justification of theistic belief. If that case succeeds, there is less need to stress, as I have, the fiduciary attitudes as central in the reconciliation of reason and religion. If the case fails, then the need is surely great.

II. Experience As a Foundation
of Rational Theistic Belief

Experiential Justification

How might experientialism apply to justification? In answering this, I shall not consider mystical experience, understood as the rapturous overpowering kind vividly described by William James in *The Varieties of Religious Experience*. While I do not deny that such experience can provide certain kinds of justification, it is too difficult to understand, and insufficiently shared, to make it a good basis for discussing experientialism. Moreover, if what I say about nonmystical experientialism is plausible, my points can be extended to apply to the forms of mystical experience most relevant to our concerns.

If we proceed on the plausible assumption that knowledge is constituted by appropriately grounded true belief, we might begin with the prima facie case of direct knowledge of something that is ordinarily knowable only through evidence or inference, such as the results of multiplying two three-digit numbers. It might be thought that if there is direct knowledge here, then there can also be directly justified beliefs of the same propositions. But that does not follow. Knowledge need not, I think, be justified belief: The idiot savant, for instance, may have non-inferential knowledge, but surely not justification, for the arithmetic answer the *first* time the calculational mechanism reveals the product. For the mechanism may be working reliably enough to generate knowledge, yet the agent will have no inductive (or other) basis for believing that it is, or for taking the automatically presented product to be correct. Hence, whatever such examples show about knowledge, they do not refute *evidentialism about justification:* the view that justified beliefs about God are impossible except on the basis of evidence.

Could one, in some other way, be directly justified in believing such religious propositions as that God is speaking to one? Would this require a sixth sense, say a mystical faculty? And would such a sense generate justification directly, or only through one's discovering adequately strong *correlations* with what is believed through reason and ordinary experience, for instance through one's religious views' enabling one to predict publicly observable events? In the latter case, the sixth sense or mystical faculty would not be a *basic* source of justification, but would justify the beliefs it produces only after earning its justificational credentials through a sufficient proportion of those beliefs being confirmed by other sources, such as perception and introspection (which presumably are basic in the sense that their capacity to ground the justifiedness of beliefs is not derivative from that of any other source of justification).

There is a way to argue for the possibility of direct justification of certain religious beliefs, without presupposing any sources of justification beyond the classically recognized ones that produce foundational beliefs: reason and experience—roughly, intuition and reflection on the one side, and, on the other, sensory experience, introspective consciousness, and memorial impressions. This approach—especially prominent in the work of philosophers in the Calvinist tradition,[23]—need not posit either mystical apprehensions, such as overpowering, ineffable, otherworldy experiences, or special divine revelations, whether in those experiences or in the presence of apparently miraculous changes in the external world. This experientialism grounds the justification of some very important religious beliefs in common kinds of experience. Religious people sometimes say that, in ordinary life, God speaks to them, they are aware of God in the beauty of nature, and they can feel God's presence. It might be thought that descriptions of these sorts are just metaphorical. But if God is, as many think, a (divine) person, these avowals might have a literal meaning.

It may be objected that these apparently religious experiences are not of, but only suggestive of, God. Perhaps all one directly hears is a special kind of voice (presumably in one's mind's ear); perhaps all one directly sees is the natural beauty which one takes to manifest God; and perhaps one simply feels a spiritual tone in one's experience. From these moves it is easy to conclude that one is at best *indirectly* justified in believing one is experiencing God. After all, one believes it inferentially—though not, to be sure, through self-conscious inference. Instead, on the basis of one's belief that the voice one hears has certain special qualities or a special authority, one automatically believes it is God's; or, on the basis of taking a beautiful scene to be too well appointed to be a mere product of natural history, one believes that its beauty is a manifestation of divine creation; and so forth.

This inferentialization of the purportedly direct religious beliefs may be too hasty. Compare perception. Suppose it is argued that even when I am in a crowded room I am still only indirectly justified in believing that there are people before me, since I believe it on the basis of believing that there are faces, clothing, etc.

Must we accept this? I think not. I do not normally even *have* these beliefs when I believe there are people before me, even if I typically do see people *by* seeing their faces and clothing, and am *disposed* to form beliefs about those objects if, say, I am asked about someone's appearance or clothing. Why must it be otherwise with beliefs about God?

A possible disanalogy—and certainly a further complexity—arises when we consider God as the (nonpropositional) object of theistic belief. It may be argued that since God is both infinite and nonphysical, one *cannot* be acquainted with God through experience. But this will not do. Even if a road were infinitely long, I could still see it by seeing part of it. Seeing a thing does not require seeing all of it, and surely seeing an infinite thing would not entail seeing its infinity. On the other hand, if it does not entail this, how might it ground knowing or justifiedly believing that the thing *is* infinite? We do not, after all, just want to be able to experience some aspect of God, significant though that might be; we want to experience it as, and be justified in taking it to be, an aspect of God. The problem is not that God is nonphysical, for it appears that the nonphysical can be experienced directly. Thus, even if in fact my introspective experience is really of something physical, say a brain process, it presumably *need* not be of something physical; and even if it must be (because of some necessary connection that might hold between the mental and the physical), it is not experience of, say, my thoughts *as* physical. Moreover, it is surely not a necessary truth that experience in general is of something physical, and this point may be all that is required for the *possibility* of experience of God. The problem, then, is apparently not that there cannot be experience, even quite unmystical experience, of God. It is (in part) that if one experiences, say, God's speaking to one, it is not clear how one could know (or justifiedly believe) that it is *God* speaking. How would one know that one was not having a merely internal experience, such as talking to oneself in a voice one thinks is God's, or even hallucinating a divine voice?

Here the perceptual analogy is again important, particularly if we are not skeptics about perceptual belief. Why would it be less likely that my experience of looking toward, say, another person, is hallucinatory? It is true that we can, with all the other senses, verify that we see a person, whereas it may be argued that God is perceptually accessible at most to sight and hearing—presumably indirectly, since God is seen *in* appropriate things and heard *through* hearing voices that are not literally God's.[24] (This holds, at any rate, if a being's voice, in a literal sense of 'voice', must be physically grounded in a physical embodiment, though even in that case, some theologians might argue that God's voice *was* physically embodied in Christ.)[25] But the force of this point about God's limited perceptibility can be exaggerated. Surely it is not true that a single-mode sense experience can be trusted only when verification by all the other senses is possible. If that were so, we could not justifiedly believe we see a beam of light that is perceptually accessible to *only* our vision.

Experientialism, the Scientific Analogy, and
Noninferential Modes of Epistemic Dependence

The challenges so far raised for experientialism about the justification of theistic belief are weighty, but probably not decisive. Let me summarize what may be the two most serious challenges and then proceed to still more difficult issues. One problem we noted concerns the psychology of religious belief. Do people ever really believe directly that, say, God is speaking to them, or is such a belief based, however unselfconsciously, on believing that the voice in question has certain characteristics, where one takes these to indicate God's speaking? This is the *inferentiality problem*. Another problem we saw—which might be called the *publicity problem*—is how the possibility of corroboration by other people is relevant. Does it, for instance, matter crucially to religious justification that not just any normal person can be expected to see God in the beauty of nature, whereas any normal person *can* be expected to see people in a crowded room or the formation of a precipitate in a test tube? Or is this contrast blunted by the marked differences in perceptual acuity we find between clearly normal people, particularly in complicated matters such as aesthetic perception in music and painting, where what is directly heard or seen nevertheless cannot be seen or heard without both practice and sensitivity?

The scientific analogy is relevant to both problems, as well as to the general question of what is required to justify theistic beliefs, inferentially or otherwise. For one thing, scientific hypotheses are widely believed to be knowable on the basis of evidence from which they do not follow, and scientific theories are widely taken to be rationally acceptable on grounds which render them only probable. What is scientifically known is not *proved* by our evidence for it, despite the frequency with which one hears of "scientific proof." Clearly, then, so far as scientific practice is a good model of cognitive rationality, an inductive, probabilistic notion of confirmation is more appropriate to theistic beliefs than a deductive notion of confirmation, verification, or proof.

On the other hand, the scientific analogy may seem to support what we might call the *standard equipment view:* the thesis that a belief is justified only if it can be confirmed by others using the same basic equipment—above all, the five senses. This view is plausible for a certain range of cases, and it probably does carry some weight against *mystical* experientialism, though mystics may certainly claim that it is their sensitivity, and not their possession of special faculties, which accounts for their extraordinary awarenesses. In any case, the standard equipment view need not pose a problem for nonmystical experientialism once it is granted that even those who share the same equipment may be quite unequally skilled in using it and utterly different in the data they are able to find even in using it to test the same propositions.

It should also be emphasized that inference to the best explanation is crucial to understanding scientific rationality. But what is an explanation, and can divine action or divine plans constitute an explanation, or partial explanation, in a sense relevant to rationality? I believe that a good case can be made for this, though the relevant kind of explanation is admittedly not experimentally testable: God is simply not accessible to controlled experiments. If, for any finite stretch of time, divine action on the world is predictable at all, what is predictable is not specifiable in terms appropriate to experimental confirmation. Granted that theists may *expect* providential events like discovering trapped coal miners alive, such expectations cannot be grounded in warranted beliefs about God that supply premises entailing, or even implying with high probability, a determinate intervention of this sort. There is a difference, however, between *experimental* and *experiential* confirmation; and the issue here is in part whether experience not based on the results of experiment can ever confirm theistic propositions. Moreover, once we distinguish clearly between confirmation and proof, indeed between gathering support by degrees and obtaining conclusive evidence, we can better characterize the various evidential relations between experience and religious views.

Experientialism raises ontological questions too. Can God be seen in, rather than so to speak inferred from, nature? This is arguable, but even if nature is conceived as God's work, it is still not partly constitutive of God, at least not in the way that the color and shape by which I see a tree presumably are in part constitutive of *it*. Or is nature, as some views have it, partly constitutive of God after all?[26] If so, then directly perceiving God may be in a way too easy, or at least quite easy to do without directly perceiving the divine aspect of what one sees or forming any justified beliefs about any such aspect. One could not see a beautiful landscape without seeing some aspect of God. One could see an aspect without seeing it *as* manifesting God; but that would be insensitivity, not perceptual inadequacy or divine elusiveness.

So far, I have tried to treat experientialism sympathetically, but I have also pointed out some difficulties for it, including the possibility that religious beliefs apparently based directly on experience might in fact be evidentially dependent, in unnoticed ways, on nonreligious beliefs. There is still another way in which evidential dependence might occur. Such religious beliefs might exhibit *historical evidential dependence:* one belief is historically evidentially dependent on a second provided that, though the first is not now justified (or a case of knowledge) in virtue of the present justification (or knowledge status) of the second (which the subject need no longer hold), its current justification (or status as knowledge) is epistemically dependent on the second belief's having been justified (or a case of knowledge). Consider one's beliefs, formed as a child, that one's elders (those who introduced one to one's religion) knew God, or at least had other religious knowledge. Could one now be noninferentially justified in one's current theistic beliefs, had one not been justified in holding beliefs acquired from one's religious elders, and if one's present belief did not trace by some appropriate route (doubtless involving memory) to those earlier ones? If not, then these current religious beliefs would be justified only on the basis of past evidence, and we would confront the question of how, initially, one's religious community came to know God.[27] A major—and controversial—Christian answer to this is well known: through the historical Jesus. As Karl Barth put one version of this view, Christ is the knowability of God.

If we consider our complicated situation in the contemporary world, still another problem besets us. We know about intelligent people who think there is insufficient ground for theistic belief, and we are aware of arguments to the effect that the problem of evil shows that it is more reasonable to disbelieve than to believe that God exists. Even if we start out nonevidentially justified in believing certain theistic propositions, do we not *now* need evidence that these detractors are wrong, for instance that theistic philosophers have refuted them? Call this the *defeasibility problem*. The point is not that our theistic beliefs come to depend positively on such evidence; the dependence is only negative: What we need is not evidential *grounds*, but evidential *protection*—such as might be provided by natural theology—against erosion of the grounds we have. But the point is that our overall justification for believing in God would still depend on evidence and so would lose the pristine purity that is attractive in certain versions of experientialism. This point should not be exaggerated, however: A source can be pure even if it must be guarded from interlopers who would poison it. Impurity may still result, however, if the strategies of protection fail—or become ends in themselves.

Suppose, finally, that we dispel all these worries and warrantedly conclude that, even without evidence of any kind, we may justifiedly hold theistic beliefs. Now the question arises whether, by appeal to apparently confirmatory sensory experience, anyone may claim as much for any favored position which is not obviously unwarranted, perhaps including religious views that are incompatible with our own. If similar experiences had by others do support religious views incompatible with our own, it is at least questionable whether our own experiences justify our religious views. This is the *permissibility problem*. It appears that the capacity of our experiences to justify us depends on our warrant for taking others not to have similar experiences that justify them in holding beliefs incompatible with ours. The solution to the problem is far from obvious. It may be argued that since the same point holds for the ordinary experiences which justify perceptual beliefs, the permissibility problem is a general skeptical difficulty; but the parallel is at least not obvious. It may also be argued that the permissibility problem only shows that the experiential justification in question is of limited degree: sufficient, perhaps, to render a theistic outlook rational, but not to warrant taking it to constitute knowledge, or to be better justified than alternatives similarly confirmed. Here it is important to remember the distinction between an internal and an external reconciliation of faith and reason: between reconciling them in the life of a religious person (or at least some kinds of religious person) and, on the other hand, providing theistic beliefs with grounds that would satisfy a skeptic, or at least provide a neutral nontheist with justification for adopting such beliefs. Perhaps there is no need for an external reconciliation, or at all events that may be far less important than internal reconciliations. And perhaps in certain matters, all one needs is a kind of justification that renders one's own view rationally permissible, not a kind that implies its preferability over competing views. Here again it may be significant that rationality is distinguishable from justification. The way is certainly open to argue that if experientialism about justification turns out to be too strong, the counterpart view about rationality is not.

On balance, it seems to me not clear that experientialism provides an adequate account of how theistic belief may be justified. But suppose it does. Its success depends on a kind of justification not possessed by, and perhaps not even available to, all religious people, including many in the Hebraic-Christian tradition. For even those who open themselves to, for instance, God's speaking to them cannot always count on his doing so or—if they believe he often does—on being honestly able to take his doing so to be what it is. Even divine deliverances might be misheard, and deep-seated desires can cause us to think we are spoken to when all we hear is our own voice in disguise. Experiential justification is relative to one's experience; and in a world of steel and concrete, of traffic noises and the blare of monotonous music and relentless advertising, of crowding and competition for scarce resources, there are many who at least cannot readily open themselves in the right way, and there are some who, despite a history of unqualifiedly held theistic beliefs, find themselves in a state in which they seem no longer open, or no longer unqualifiedly believe the religious propositions they once did. For all that, these people can have nondoxastic religious faith, and any experiences that count toward justification of their believing the same propositions will count—and weigh more heavily—toward justification of nondoxastic faith regarding those propositions. Indeed, nondoxastic faith may sometimes be a precondition for the experiences that may justify theistic belief; it may certainly develop an openness to them. How might the faith, and indeed the overall religious commitment, of people in these positions be rational?

III. The Possibility of Rational Faith

Fiduciary Versus Doxastic Theistic Attitudes

In view of the defeasibility and permissibility problems, and given the difficulties directly confronting experientialism itself, it becomes quite important whether we are assessing theistic *belief* or other theistic attitudes. I have already argued that the standards of justification and rationality appropriate to faith and hope are less stringent. One might have strong faith in God and accompanying propositional faith that God is, say, sovereign, without actually believing that this is so, yet also without in any way doubting it. I propose, then, to concentrate on what I have been calling nondoxastic faith. Some propositional faith *is* doxastic; but much is not, and even in religious contexts there is nothing abnormal about having faith that, say, God loves all human beings, without believing that this is so. Think of the problem of evil.

Nondoxastic faith may seem too pale to sustain a religious life. One might object that such faith comes to no more than weak belief and deserves no higher place as an element in religious commitment. But nondoxastic faith is surely not equivalent to weak belief. Even flat-out belief can be weak, in the usual sense that it is not marked by conviction and, even more important, is not strongly entrenched or highly resistant to dissipation through forgetting or to collapse in a confrontation with apparent counterevidence. Neither point need apply to nondoxastic faith. As I understand such faith, say faith that God is sovereign, it is quite compatible with a general posture of *religious conviction*, which I take to be a matter of such things as the overall strength of one's faith,[28] the depth of one's resolution to try to quell doubts one may have about God's sovereignty and goodness, and the extent of one's determination to make one's religious outlook central in one's life.[29] It is quite consistent with the nondoxastic character of the faith that it be strong both in the extent to which it pervades one's life and in its resistance to being forgotten or given up too readily upon discovery of counterevidence.

Unlike belief, nondoxastic faith does not represent a definitely *accepted propositional object;* but, in the role it gives to its *projected propositional object*, it may far exceed belief. There is a sense in which the person of nondoxastic (propositional) faith and the person unqualifiedly believing the same proposition have the same picture of the world; but they differ in their relation to that picture. To unpack some of the metaphor, there are at least three areas of difference: those of avowal of the proposition, inferences from it, and nonverbal behavior on the basis of it. If—as is often not the case—other things are equal, belief implies stronger dispositions to avow the proposition, to draw inferences from it, and to act on it.

Nondoxastic faith is also highly consonant with a kind of theistic *trust,* and at least when well developed this faith implies an attitude of trust in God, by which I mean in part a sense that God has seen to it, or will see to it, that ultimately things turn out as they should.[30] Note the similarities between 'I have faith that' and 'I trust that'. I take nondoxastic faith to imply (though it goes beyond) a kind of cognitive trusting. Wholehearted devotion to God is possible through such faith, even though unqualified theistic belief is not entailed by it. Religious conviction implies some cognitive commitments, yet not necessarily theistic beliefs; and an associated nondoxastic faith, while it does not embody beliefs of propositions self-evidently entailing God's existence, does embody the kinds of beliefs required to understand one's religion and its implications for conduct, for instance beliefs about the divine nature and the implications of one's religion for daily life. If evidentialism is wrong even for religious faith, including nondoxastic faith—or if, alternatively, its evidential demands could be met by faith—that would be very significant. Let us pursue this idea.

Suppose evidentialists are right in insisting that, for cognitive religious commitments—including nondoxastic fiduciary commitments—justification, and even rationality, requires evidence. Still, the kind and amount required would differ for faith as opposed to belief. Theists tend to want to refute evidentialism across the board, for all the (normal) cognitive religious attitudes.

But the rationality of religious commitment does not require doing so, even if—as I am supposing for the sake of argument—evidential considerations are insufficient to justify theistic beliefs. Nondoxastic religious faith might be warranted, whether experientially or evidentially, even where religious belief is not. Call this view of the rationality of cognitive religious commitment *the nondoxastic approach*. I say 'cognitive' because, while the view stops short of claiming (though it leaves open) that theistic belief is justified, it is cognitive in taking faith—at least faith *that*—to have propositional objects. It may indeed have the same propositional objects as the beliefs which experientialists take to be justified by religious experience, and it typically will have some of them, such as that God is present in certain moments of deep emotion, or on occasions of gratuitous-seeming sustenance in the face of stress. This view thus contrasts with noncognitivism, on which religious utterances are expressive of attitudes and feelings, but not semantically affirmational in a sense implying the expression of truth or falsehood.

There are at least two important objections to this nondoxastic, fiduciary approach which we should consider immediately. One is direct and challenges the truth of the nondoxastic view. The second challenges the adequacy of the view to the cognitive aspects of religious commitment.

The direct challenge is straightforward. If you are justified in having faith, but not belief, regarding a proposition, then from your perspective its negation is more probable than it (not in the sense that you must believe the negation—as a theist would surely not—but in the sense that your total relevant evidence justifies you in believing it). Otherwise, you would be justified in believing, even if in a tentative spirit, that it is true. But if, from your perspective, its negation is more probable than it, you are not justified in believing it. I deny the main premise: We are talking about justification, not probability; and justification for faith that, say, God loves us, implies no ascription of a probability to the proposition, nor even of a range of probabilities. This holds at least equally for rationality as applied to the relevant theistic attitudes, and there is no need for a separate discussion of rationality. Moreover, insofar as justification for nondoxastic faith may imply justification for ascribing a probability to the proposition in question, it would be one greater than .50; hence, unwillingness to assign it to a theistic proposition would not imply that one should assign the proposition a probability *lower* than .50. In any case, the kind of justification we are considering is not only such as to make it rationally permissible to believe; it is also the sort of justification which, when possessed by a true belief, normally renders it knowledge. If this sort of justification—or the weaker counterpart notion of rationality—can be understood in terms of probability at all, it is still not clear how to assign degrees of probability in the special case of theistic beliefs. We cannot play dice with the universe in that way.

The second objection is this. Supposing that justified theistic faith is possible even where justified belief is not, the nondoxastic view may still fail to do justice to religious commitment. How, it may be asked, can I center my life on a view not even really believed? The question is worrisome. But notice two points. First, religious behavior can flow from nondoxastic faith just as it can from belief: A cognitively projected conception of the world can structure one's behavior in essentially the same way that a flatly accepted conception can. This is in part because—and here is the second point by way of reply—a kind of conviction is quite possible without belief: One can, for instance, grant that one does not know or flatly believe that God exists, and that only one's faith is justified, without lacking a sense of surety, even a kind of certitude, about many aspects of God. For instance, regarding God's sovereignty over life and death, one might have an attitude of certitude about the appropriateness of conceiving human life under the aspect of divine governance. The existential propositions about God are objects of rational faith and not of belief; but normative propositions about God and many concerning how life should be lived in a world under God are believed, and may be strongly believed. Even if one's theistic picture of the world is expressed by a fiduciary projection, and not by a set of believed propositions, one may unqualifiedly and rationally believe that the world so conceived, and human life conducted in accord with that conception, are good. Neither cognitive commitment to the goodness of the picture, nor a steadfast resolve to promote it and act as it requires, entails believing the projection to be correct.

It might seem that this view substitutes a certainty that theism is *probably* true for a conviction that it *is* true. That is not so. While this probability belief is consistent with nondoxastic faith, having the belief is not what that faith comes to, nor does nondoxastic faith even imply a probability belief of this kind. A person who does not have a flat-out belief that God exists might find it inappropriate to say, and might neither believe nor disbelieve, that probably God exists. Moreover, nondoxastic faith can carry a conviction that the world is to be viewed as God's domain, and a deep, perhaps even unshakable, commitment to the hope that this is so, without the subject's having any probability beliefs on the matter. It is indeed possible to be religious without ever forming probability beliefs about such ultimate matters. Certainly their formation is not essential to a religious outlook.

A third reply deserves special emphasis. Because it is natural to say, publicly as well as privately, what one religiously holds, and because we typically do believe flat-out—and often think we know—what we put forward as our stance on a major matter, it is odd, even disconcerting, to think of religious views, or at least those central in a religious commitment, as not unqualifiedly believed. But this discomfort can be relieved. Religious affirmation must not be assimilated to ordinary or even scientific factual assertion. If there is a scientific analogue, it is *theoretical* assertion, which also does not entail belief and is often accompanied by a fallibilistic awareness that one does not know the proposition in question to be true. Moreover, avowal need not rest on evidence or proof in order to be rational. And embracing a view as central in one's life may be warranted even apart from evidence sufficient to justify flat-out belief that it is true.

Once again, it is essential to prevent skepticism from biasing our conception of rationality. Just as, if we talk about what knowledge is while skepticism lies in our peripheral vision, we tend to set our standards too high, or to require of ourselves a capacity to *show* we know as a condition of knowing itself, so when we talk about the rationality of our religious outlook with the *assertive paradigm* in the background, we tend both to set our standard of rationality high and to require, as a condition for rationally holding our outlook, the ability to justify it to an uncommitted outsider. Even perceptual justification will not, in general, stand this second-order demand and can be distorted by the self-conscious standard we may adopt in the attempt to light our way out of the skeptical shadows. The rationality of religious belief should be analogously understood.

None of these points is meant to suggest that flat-out theistic belief is inappropriate as a part of religious commitment. Indeed, doubtless there is, in many cases, at least, a kind of courage that is lacking in a religious person who cannot hold such theistic beliefs. My point has been that they are not required for faith and are subject to different and more stringent criteria of rationality. A kind of faith that does not entail belief, then, is a more appropriate attitude for many of those who are concerned with the rationality of their religious outlook. Above all, the possibility of such faith sets a different baseline for religious rationality (in the cognitive domain) than would be appropriate if the counterpart beliefs were a necessary condition for religious commitment.

If there is one way in which this fiduciary approach attenuates the cognitive aspect of religious commitment, there is also a respect in which it heightens the volitional dimension. If you take your grounds for a view to be conclusive, you normally have no choice but to accept it. When you embrace a faith (partly) on the basis of indications you believe significant but far from conclusive, you may rationally choose to take some cognitive risk, hoping for further confirmation and allowing the faith to nurture the hope, while the hope—leading to an open-minded search—may reinforce the faith. In this sense, faith that is aware of its own risks, and is nurtured by a steadfast religious devotion, can express a kind of religious commitment not possible for those to whom religious truths are obvious. Single-mindedness can be in tension with wholeheartedness. One can choose, and retain, one's religious commitment more freely when its rational grounds are less obvious and do not seem compelling.[31]

I do not mean to imply that there cannot be directly justified or, more modestly, directly rational religious beliefs. I leave this possibility open. It is at best very difficult to establish absolute restrictions on what sorts of beliefs can be directly justified or directly rational. This holds even if the only way beliefs can be directly justified or rational is by virtue of their noninferential grounding in the four basic sources of justification widely countenanced in the epistemological tradition. In any case, I have stressed that faith, though it is, by virtue of its propositional objects, cognitive, need not be, by virtue of entailing belief, doxastic; and even if there should be few if any experientially justified theistic beliefs, there may yet be experientially justified religious faith.

A parallel point holds for absolute restrictions on what we can justifiably believe (or know) on the basis of one or more arguments or in some less explicitly evidential way, as where, without any process of inference, a belief simply develops on the basis of other beliefs one has which express grounds for it. It is especially difficult to determine what can be justifiedly believed (or known) through a combination of plausible but individually inconclusive arguments for the same conclusion. As both coherentists and modest foundationalists are at pains to show, a belief may be justified not only by grounding in one or more conclusive arguments, but also by its support from—which implies some degree of coherence with—many sets of independent premises none of which, alone, would suffice to justify it. And again, less support is required to justify faith than to justify belief.

Admittedly, it is often hard in practice to distinguish, even in our own case, between belief or faith that is grounded directly in one of the basic experiential or rational sources, and belief or faith grounded indirectly in those sources: grounded either through other beliefs of which we may not even be aware, or through unselfconscious inference from beliefs of which we are aware. We often do not know, and frequently cannot even readily find out, why we believe what we do, especially when there are multiple considerations that incline us to hold the belief in question. Thus, what we take to be a direct belief may really be based on at least one other belief and may depend for its justification on the evidence or grounds expressed by some other belief. If, however, there cannot be directly justified religious beliefs of the kind we have been discussing, it might still be true that there can be direct knowledge of such propositions; and for some religious people, even knowledge without justification would count as very precious in this case. It would, perhaps, count as one kind of faith.[32] But it would be very different from faith as usually conceived, and certainly would be a kind of doxastic faith. The point I am making is that even a strong faith which is sufficiently rooted in a person to form the center of a religious life, need not be doxastic.

Rationality and Religious Conduct: The Behavioral Dimension of Religious Commitment

Before closing I want to return to the point that much of religious commitment is not cognitive in any narrow sense: While beliefs or nondoxastic fiduciary attitudes may in some way underlie it, it consists in dispositions to conduct oneself in a certain way, in and outside one's specifically religious life. Consider examples from two representative domains, the moral and the aesthetic.

Suppose my religious faith is in a God whom I take to command altruism and justice. Can my faith, if itself justified, justify my acting accordingly? I think it can, at least where I do not have good reason to abstain from the conduct in question. To be sure, my moral actions so motivated would, if other things are equal, be more extensively justified if I had enough justification for beliefs of the relevant theistic propositions; but that point is consistent with the modest degree of fiduciary justification in question here. What holds for justification seems also to hold for rationality, and the examples to follow concerning the former can be readily applied to the latter.

There is another point of the first importance: Rational persons normally have moral grounds for ethical conduct—both for being ethical in general and for the morally obligatory actions they actually perform—that are (in my view) justificationally independent of theistic commitments. Usually, these grounds are themselves sufficient to warrant the relevant moral acts, in this case the altruistic and just actions. Indeed, even if this justificational overdetermination did not hold, by and large rational persons should make some effort to find all of (or at least a goodly number of) the available major justifying grounds for important kinds of conduct they engage in, particularly if it is controversial. This not only yields better justified conduct; it also helps one both to understand one's obligations and to fulfill them. It clarifies precisely what one should on balance do; it often provides a sense of why one should do it; and it strengthens one's motivation to do it.

Similar points hold in the aesthetic case. A cathedral built as a beautiful monument to God can also be constructed so that it serves secular community needs sufficiently pressing to justify such a construction in their own right; and a rational builder will certainly try to make it safe enough to avoid crushing the huddled families who may take shelter there during storms. To be sure, the demands of beauty can conflict with those of utility, and a rational religious person can then face agonizing conflicts. But nondoxastic faith is no worse off than belief in such conflicts. Indeed, one lesson of history is that if people do not regard their theistic beliefs and other religious beliefs as infallible or unassailably justified, there is a better chance of reconciling them with secular considerations—or other religious views—that tend in a different direction.

The importance of these points goes beyond their calling attention to secular sources of justification for conduct, and for related attitudes, central in the lives of the religious. One of the main reasons why we worry about the rationality of religious commitment is the fear that if it is not rational, then much of the basis of many human lives, and much human conduct, is left without rational foundation. A motivational and attitudinal foundation for the conduct in question would often remain; but even if such a foundation were stable, it would not be rational. I have tried to speak directly to this worry. At least in the case of the Hebraic-Christian tradition, there are secular reasons sufficient both to justify and to motivate the core of the Christian moral commitment and most though of course not all of the obligatory interpersonal attitudes. This applies to the centrality of love, to a version of the moral directives in the Ten Commandments, and to much that Jesus taught by example. The point does not in general apply to behavior called for by the distinctive theological commitments of a particular religion, such as patterns of worship and ritual. But if the moral attitudes in question are accepted by adherents of differing religions, we may reasonably hope that there will be ample support for mutual toleration of these differences in religious commitments.

If there is no antidote to skepticism about cognitive religious attitudes, the sting of that skepticism is greatly relieved when we grasp how much secular justification can be brought to bear in supporting the same nonreligious attitudes and religiously neutral behavior that are among the central manifestations of much religious commitment: love of one's neighbor, charity toward the poor, the quest for world peace. This holds even if, psychologically, the agents in question are motivated by religious convictions more strongly than by secular ones, such as the moral beliefs which they realize also support their conduct.[33]

Conclusion

My conception of the rationality of religious commitment is holistic. It is a commitment of the heart and not just the head, of a lifetime and not just its sabbaths. It affects one's moral and interpersonal conduct, as well as one's attitudes toward the universe and toward human existence within it. The rationality of this commitment, particularly for those in whom nondoxastic faith is fundamental, does not reduce to that of religious belief. The same holds for the justification of religious commitment, which is not equivalent to nor entailed by its rationality. The justification of faith, for instance, does not reduce to that of the religious beliefs. Nor is the rationality of one's cognitive religious position by any means the only element in the rationality of one's overall religious commitment. Conduct, attitudes, and emotions are also part of the pattern to be appraised.

Even if a religious commitment is central in one's life, it need not conflict with one's commitments as a rational agent simpliciter, and secular considerations may cooperate with religious ones in supporting moral and other conduct we think of as rational. The cooperation may be psychological, by virtue of religious and secular sources each providing motivation for certain conduct, as well as evidential, by way of each supplying justificatory grounds for certain behavior and attitudes. It is not clear to what extent experience, or arguments, can justify, or at least render rational, one's holding religious beliefs; but there are surely some lives in which the character of experience, in the context of the overall intellectual outlook, justifies, or renders rational, at least theistic faith. I doubt that an account of rational religious commitment should demand more as a minimal condition of rationality, natural though it is to impose stricter standards of rationality given the importance of the life commitments that are at stake.

Rational religious commitment lies somewhere between a headlong confidence in what we passionately wish to be true and a timid refusal to risk disappointments, between the safety of according to religious beliefs the easy confidence we have in the things that bombard the five senses, and the detachment that comes from suspending judgment on whatever is not plainly evident to all, between a merely aesthetic participation in religious practices and a dogmatic doctrinal codification of one's outlook on the world, between noncognitivist attenuation of religious texts and rigid literalism in understanding them, between apathy and conformism, between skepticism and credulity. Rational religious commitment may be elusive; it differs in many ways from one person to another; and, even in a single life, it may change much over time, for better or for worse. But if our notion of rationality is not too narrow, if our sense of the interconnection between the religious and the secular is sufficiently keen, and if we do not try to justify needlessly strong cognitive attitudes, we may well be able to construct an adequate theory of rational religious commitment and thereby progress toward a better reconciliation of faith and reason.

Notes

Acknowledgments: This essay has benefited from discussions with various audiences, particularly at Wake Forest University's James Montgomery Hester Seminar in 1989, where the exchange of ideas with my co-symposiasts, William Alston, Terence Penelhum, and Richard Popkin, was of much help in doing the final revisions. An earlier version was delivered in part at the University of Chicago Divinity School; parts of an intermediate version were given at Davidson College, the University of Mississippi, and the University of Nebraska; and in a number of places the essay draws on my "Faith, Belief, and Rationality," *Philosophical Perspectives* 5 (1991), written during the same period and delivered at Georgetown University as the Aquinas Lecture in 1989. For detailed comments on earlier versions, I thank William Alston, Roger Ebertz, James Gustafson, Allison Nespor, Louis Pojman, William L. Rowe, Calvin Schrag, James Sennett, and William Lad Sessions.

1. It is noteworthy that Robert M. Adams begins an excellent essay on faith with puzzlement about how faith can be regarded as a virtue given that "(1) Belief and unbelief seem to be mainly involuntary states, and it is thought that the involuntary cannot be ethically praised or blamed. (2) If belief is to be praised at all, we are accustomed to think that its praiseworthiness depends on its rationality, but the virtuousness of faith for Christians seems to be based on its correctness and independent of the strength of the evidence for it." See "The Virtue of Faith," in his *The Virtue of Faith* (New York: Oxford University Press, 1987), p. 9 (originally published in *Faith and Philosophy* 1 [1984]). While in the same essay he takes up the element of trust often taken to belong to faith, he is here speaking of faith as a kind of belief, and indeed elsewhere says that "Kierkegaard is surely right in placing religious faith in the category of beliefs for which 'probably' is not enough." See "The Leap of Faith," in Adams, *The Virtue of Faith*, p. 45. I shall speak later to this doxastic con-

ception of faith; and while I cannot take up the two problems Adams raises concerning faith as a virtue, I hope that the position I propose leaves us in a good position to deal with them.

2. For a brief discussion of how skepticism tends to focus our attention on second-order justification and knowledge and to encourage confusion between the first- and the second-order cases, see my *Belief, Justification, and Knowledge* (Belmont, Calif.: Wadsworth, 1988), esp. chap. 9. On that topic and in the assessment of evidentialism and the experientialist opposition to it, this essay draws on that work, esp. the third section of chap. 8.

3. William P. Alston has been a persistent critic of this move. See his *Epistemic Justification* (Ithaca, N.Y.: Cornell University Press, 1989), esp. chap. 6, "Level Confusions in Epistemology." An account of some important truths that are distorted by the move is suggested in my "Justification, Truth, and Reliability," *Philosophy and Phenomenological Research* 49 (1988).

4. There is, to be sure, a commonsense strain in Hume, and in following it he talks (in the *Enquiry*) of "the authority of experience" and suggests that we may "justly" infer propositions about the future from certain others about the past. I am talking about the skeptical Hume, though even here I do not mean to imply that his main focus was justification rather than, say, knowledge or certainty.

5. I am ignoring the a priori here, in part for simplicity and in part because, as applied to our beliefs of propositions reasonably considered a priori, skepticism is less plausible. Moreover, historically skeptics have been less inclined to focus their attack on such beliefs. This issue is treated briefly in my "Justification, Truth, and Reliability."

6. In "The Architecture of Reason," *Proceedings and Addresses of the American Philosophical Association* 62 (1988) and "Rationalization and Rationality," *Synthese* 65 (1985), I have discussed in detail both the nature of rationality and its structural parallel with justification.

7. The influence of science on our understanding of rationality, and some of the common distortions arising from mistaken views about science, are discussed in my "Realism, Rationality, and Philosophical Method," *Proceedings and Addresses of the American Philosophical Association* 61 (1987).

8. One stereotype that must be rejected is the view that scientific hypotheses or theories are proved. For a classical account of what is wrong with this view, see Pierre Duhem, *The Aim and Structure of Physical Theory*,

trans. Philip P. Wiener (New York: Atheneum, 1962). A short presentation of the point that scientific hypotheses are not established by proof,
distinguishing confirmation from proof, is given in my essay "The Sci-
ences and the Humanities," *National Forum* 18 (1983).

9. Process theologians, such as Charles Hartshorne, deny that God is
omnipotent in the traditional sense. For a sympathetic theological treatment of some of the pertinent issues which engages Hartshorne's views
at various points, see David Tracy, *Blessed Rage for Order* (Minneapolis:
Winston Seabury Press, 1975), esp. chap. 8. Cf. James M. Gustafson's
conception of God as a power that bears down upon us; the conception
does not seem meant to imply omnipotence (if indeed it is compatible
with agency, which is plausibly thought to be implicit in omnipotence).
See James M. Gustafson, *Ethics from a Theocentric Perspective*, vol. 1 (Chicago: University of Chicago Press, 1981).

10. For a short statement of the picture preference view of religious
avowal, see Anthony Flew's contribution to the Symposium on Theology
and Falsification in Anthony Flew and Alasdair MacIntyre, eds., *New
Essays in Philosophical Theology* (London: SCM Press, 1955). R. M. Hare
offers a different noncognitivist view in the same place. John Hick's reply
to Flew, in "Theology and Verification," *Theology Today* 17 (1960), is interesting in itself and has generated much discussion.

11. The importance of hope as a religious attitude is developed by
James Muyskens in *The Sufficiency of Hope* (Philadelphia: Temple University Press, 1979) and discussed in detail by Louis P. Pojman in *Religious
Belief and the Will* (London and New York: Routledge and Kegan Paul,
1986). Pojman also argues cogently for the importance of other religious
attitudes and offers a conception of religious faith as hope. See esp.
chap. 16. Cf. James Muyskens, "What Is Virtuous About Faith?" *Faith
and Philosophy* 2 (1985), and Robert Solomon's treatment of hope as faith:
"Hope is faith uncertain, a passive anticipation of a positive fortune, beyond one's own control but always possible." See Robert Solomon, *The
Passions* (New York: Doubleday, 1976), p. 327.

12. I hold that believing a proposition is not equivalent to believing it
to be (or that it is) true, and that, especially in discussions with someone
whom one finds credible, one can accept something as true and not believe it. Much more could be said about belief, but nothing I say should
turn on aspects of the notion left unresolved here. When I speak of taking
as true, I do not mean having the semantic belief that the proposition is

true, but something like treating the proposition as one does what one believes to be true, for instance as a basis of inference.

13. I introduced and defended this distinction in "Believing and Affirming," *Mind* 91 (1982).

14. Cf. L. J. Cohen's view that "Faith (in the everyday sense) that God exists is an example of belief, not acceptance," where "to accept that p is to have or adopt a policy of claiming positing or postulating that p . . ." and "Belief that p on the other hand, is a disposition to feel it true that p, whether or not one goes along with the proposition as a premise." See L. J. Cohen, "Belief and Acceptance," *Mind* 98 (1989), p. 386. I reject the suggested assimilation of propositional faith to belief, but it seems to me that such faith *is* something like what Cohen (mistakenly, I think) says belief is. Joseph Runzo quite explicitly treats faith *that* as "basically equivalent to the cognitive state of belief," though on other points his treatment of the distinction between propositional and attitudinal faith is consistent with my construal of it. See his "World-Views and the Epistemic Foundations of Theism," *Religious Studies* 25 (1990): 44.

15. I am distinguishing between separate beliefs of contradictories and beliefs of a contradiction. The case against the possibility of the former seems less strong than that against the possibility of the latter, but I leave its possibility open. Perhaps we should, for similar reasons, leave open the possibility of having faith that p even while disbelieving it. It may be, however, that faith is dominant in a way belief is not, so that genuine faith that p rules out the kind of negative attitude toward p implicit in disbelieving it.

16. Compare Pojman's denial that "belief-in statements entail belief-that statements" and his suggestion that "if belief-in, or trusting, can be analyzed in terms of commitment to a course of action or a disposition to act, then it seems that we do not need to believe-that x exists in order to believe-in or deeply hope in the existence of x" (Pojman, *Religious Belief*, p. 224). I agree with much of what Pojman says on this topic but am inclined to take belief in God to entail, by virtue of presupposing, a cognitive commitment to God's existence. Since I do not take every kind of religious trust to entail this (such as trust regarding the occurrence of future states of affairs as prayed for), I would not treat belief in God as equivalent to religious trust (though the former implies the latter), but I agree with Pojman that, like hope, such trust does not entail what I call flat-out belief that God exists (or beliefs self-evidently entailing this, such

as that God loves us). Granted, taken literally, trusting God, like trusting any being, entails the existence of the object of trust; I am assuming that there is a kind of religious trust that is not relational in this way. It is an attitude of trust regarding states of affairs associated with God and could be internal to the faithful person.

17. Faith and hope also have noncognitive components and in that way are more complex than belief. Faith implies a certain kind of positive attitude toward its object, and hope that something will occur is widely taken to imply wanting to some degree that it occur.

18. I say "ultimately" because there can be an indefinitely long sequence of defeaters and defeaters of the defeaters, and what matters is the end result. An even number leaves the original justification intact.

19. They only tend to create knowledge because there are cases in which the justification, whatever its degree, is the wrong kind to render a true belief knowledge. For instance, even if I justifiedly and truly believe my ticket will lose a sweepstakes with a million coupons and one winner, I do not know that it will. Nor do I acquire knowledge that it will lose if the number of coupons increases, even though my belief gains proportionately in probability.

20. This is defended indirectly in my *Belief, Justification, and Knowledge* and directly in my "The Architecture of Reason."

21. For a valuable discussion of the nonevidential role of arguments for God's existence, see Nicholas Wolterstorff, "The Migration of the Theistic Arguments: From Natural Theology to Evidentialist Apologetics," in *Rationality, Religious Belief, and Moral Commitment: New Essays in the Philosophy of Religion*, ed. Robert Audi and William J. Wainwright (Ithaca, N.Y.: Cornell University Press, 1986).

22. This raises the question whether the relevant arguments might be combined into a single cogent one. It should not be assumed that the combination process would, in any simple way, preserve evidential cogency; but in any event the resulting conjunctive premise might be too complex to be grasped, or at least appreciated, as a whole, and the subject might thus be unable to derive justification for the conclusion on the basis of that conjunction.

23. One might also call it the Calvinian tradition, given how many of its leading figures have been associated with Calvin College. For an extensive statement of Alvin Plantinga's antievidentialist approach, see his "Reason and Belief in God," in *Faith and Rationality*, ed. Alvin Plantinga and Nicholas Wolterstorff (Notre Dame: University of Notre Dame

Press, 1983). William P. Alston has developed a different but complementary case for an experiential basis of religious belief, and a short statement is given in his "The Perception of God," *Philosophical Topics* 16 (1988). Cf. his "Perceiving God," *The Journal of Philosophy* 83 (1986). Plantinga's approach is critically discussed in my "Direct Justification, Evidential Dependence, and Theistic Belief," in *Rationality, Religious Belief, and Moral Commitment*, ed. Audi and Wainwright, and the papers in that collection by Kenneth Konyndyk, Ralph McInerny, Alvin Plantinga, and Nicholas Wolterstorff also bear on the issue.

24. This is certainly controversial. For a powerful case against it, and a great deal of argument for the possibility of various kinds of perceptual experiences of God, see William P. Alston, *Perceiving God* (Ithaca, N.Y.: Cornell University Press, 1991).

25. Cf. Isaiah 6:8–9, "And I heard the voice of the Lord saying, 'Whom shall I send, and who will go for us?' " There is little question that the voice is taken to be physically heard, and perhaps God is even conceived as physically (if indirectly) touched, depending on whether God's embodiment may be thought to extend to the touch of the sacred coal.

26. Here one might compare John Calvin's extraordinary statement that "it can be said reverently . . . that nature is God" provided one does not confuse God with the "inferior course of his works." This is quoted and discussed in James M. Gustafson, *Ethics from a Theocentric Perspective* (Chicago: University of Chicago Press, 1981), 1:258.

27. A possible reply here is that one's past experience need only have supplied one with the concept of God; one's experiential justification may apparently presuppose this without historical evidential dependence. I cannot properly assess this view here; but it should be noted that because of the kind of being God is (particularly because he is infinite and in some sense transcendent), it would seem that in order to form noninferentially justified beliefs of the relevant kind, such as that he is speaking to one, one needs not only a concept of him, but also at least some justified beliefs about how he appears or what human experiences actually represent him.

28. The overall strength of one's faith is not to be identified with the closeness of its cognitive component to certainty or, closely related to that, the degree of probability one is disposed to assign. This is just one dimension, and faith can be strong overall even if not in this respect.

29. Cf. Pojman's statement that "to believe-in God implies only that one regards such a being as possibly existing and that one is committed to

live *as if* such a being does exist" (*Religious Belief*, p. 227). My conception is stronger in at least one way: The cognitive commitment to possibility is too weak (though Pojman does not have in mind here mere logical possibility). Depending on what it is to live as if God exists, my view may be stronger in a second way; for instance, one's reasons for religiously motivated action will not come from a kind of hypothetical commitment, but from a largely unconditional (though nondoxastic) commitment to one's religious view of the world. Compare living as if a missing spouse is alive. There are many ways to unpack this, and I am stressing that the merely behavioral intepretation (involving not marrying again), the interpretation with too weak a cognitive commitment (say, merely believing it possible that one's spouse is alive), and the calculative (Pascalian) reading (one will do better, in case of her return, if one can believe her return is forthcoming) are not adequate to the view I am developing (if indeed any reductive interpretation is adequate).

30. Two points are in order here. First, I say "ultimately" because, owing to evils such as those due to abuses of human freedom, things may not work out in the short run. Second, I do not speak of trusting God because I take this relationally, and so as obviously entailing God's existence.

31. This is not meant to imply that by choice one can directly determine what one will believe. But one can choose how one will lead the religious dimensions of one's live, and one can at least indirectly influence the attitudes one will take and, by these and other routes, indirectly influence one's beliefs.

32. One might deny that faith that something is so is ever compatible with knowing it is. Kant said that he had to deny knowledge of God in order to make room for faith, and certainly faith is normally contrasted with knowledge. But where one lacks a sense of knowing, or even of having good evidence, it would be natural to say one has faith rather than that one knows, and perhaps in some such cases, it is appropriate to speak so. As I understand (propositional) faith, however, it is at least not normally conceived as compatible with knowing the proposition in question. The Thomistic tradition on this matter is quite different. For valuable discussions of these issues see W. L. Sessions, "Kant and Religious Belief," *Kant-Studien* 71 (1980) and Terence Penelhum, "The Analysis of Faith in St. Thomas Aquinas," in *Faith*, ed. Terence Penelhum (New York: Macmillan, 1989).

33. I take it that a consideration justifies an action or propositional

attitude only if the action or attitude is at least in part causally sustained or produced by it, but adequate justification may be derived from a consideration even if it is not a main reason for what it justifies. For discussion of a variety of cases of multiple reasons for an action and their connection with justification see my "Acting for Reasons," *The Philosophical Review* 85 (1986) and "Rationalization and Rationality," cited in note 6.

3

PARITY IS NOT ENOUGH

In this essay I want to look at an influential argument that has been offered recently in favor of the rationality of belief in God. I want to look at it in two ways: I shall comment on its philosophical and apologetic merits and shortcomings, and I shall compare it with arguments for and against its conclusion that can be found in ancient, and particularly in early modern, philosophers. It is easier to do the one or the other separately, but I hope some useful instruction can come from the attempt to combine them here. I have a strong preference in philosophical argument for the use of proper names rather than the reference to battling "isms," even though I have been guilty of the latter now and again. It also happens in the present case that all the major positions I shall be discussing have well-known historical representatives.

I.

In recent philosophy of religion there has been a lively revival of natural theology. There have been several attempts to resuscitate the Ontological Proof;[1] there have also been vigorous and sophisticated re-presentations of the Cosmological and Teleological proofs.[2] But this revival has been balanced, and to a large extent upstaged, by another form of apologetic that has generated more interest. One of its main planks is the denigration of natural theology as traditionally practiced. Some of this denigration has even come from the philosophers who have themselves produced the putative proofs.[3] They obviously do not believe that such proofs are impossible; they think, rather, that they have no apologetic value.

Their reason for thinking this is that they fear that engaging in natural theology is likely to be the result of a damaging concession to unbelievers. This is the concession that if proofs were not available, belief in God would be irrational, because it lacked justification. This concession is one they think should not be made. They join with colleagues who do not believe proofs of God's existence are available in holding that, available or not, they are not necessary for theistic beliefs to be rational, or in some sense justified. They contend that theistic belief can be rational, or at least prima facie justified, even if it is not inferred from other beliefs in the way natural theologians have tried to infer it; it is *properly basic*. I shall call this the Basic Belief Apologetic. All the versions of it known to me take a form that at least looks as though it could be used to defend the rationality of other beliefs too. Indeed, a key part of the Apologetic includes the claim that when critics of theism insist on external support for beliefs about God, they are applying a double standard, since they are demanding satisfaction of a condition that is not imposed universally because it cannot be. There must, after all, be some beliefs that are not inferred from others, on pain of circularity or infinite regress.

This kind of apologetic is clearly topical: It is a special application of a widespread disillusionment with what is commonly called foundationalism. I take this to be the view that beliefs are only rational, or justifiable, if they can be inferred from beliefs of an epistemically privileged sort, or if they already belong to such a privileged class. The apologists who concern me claim that this disillusionment enables us to see that beliefs about God may be rational or justified even though they are not supported by the sort of external arguments proffered by natural theologians. For the same must be said of a great many nontheistic beliefs that we all have if we are not philosophical skeptics (and may only pretend not to have if we are). To require such external support in the theistic cases, while being content to do without it in what we may call the commonsense cases, is to apply a double standard— to be guilty of what Alston has called epistemic chauvinism.

I have a good deal of sympathy with this form of apologetic, but, for reasons that will appear later, I think it establishes less than its practitioners seem to think. In this essay I want to look at it in the light of some previous episodes in the history of philosophy. While I believe very deeply that every philosopher must be judged by his or her own arguments, I also believe that comparisons with analogous disputes can suggest fruitful contributions to present controversies. In this instance, I think such comparisons lend extra weight to the view that although this form of apologetic has genuine strength, it does not cast doubt on the value of natural theology but makes success in it a matter of greater apologetic urgency. I shall do nothing here to show that such success is possible, or that it is not.

II.

I am assisted in the historical task I have undertaken by a recent contribution from a resourceful representative of the mode of apologetic I have been describing. I quote the conclusion of an essay on Thomas Reid, written by Nicholas Wolterstorff:

> I have spoken of our situation as one in which philosophers have learned, as part of the rise of meta-epistemology, to question the epistemological vision by which the West has mainly lived—that of classical foundationalism. There are features of our contemporary situation which go much deeper than that, however. We live in a time when the impulses of the Enlightenment have almost played themselves out. In this situation, I sense that people are willing to ask anew about the relation between reason and revelation. Reid's Enlightenment insistence that revelation must be tested by reason no longer seems obviously true to us. Why is it that one must first run an evidential test on Scripture

before one is justified in accepting it? Does this not funda-
mentally subordinate revelation to reason? What then is left
of the authority of Scripture? But is it not fundamental to the
identity and the direction of the Christian community that
Scripture function as canon within it—that it be accepted as
authoritative? These are fundamental questions which we,
in our situation, must ask anew.[4]

In the essay that this passage concludes, Wolterstorff gives an
approving account of Reid's answer to Hume's skepticism. As
Wolterstorff describes him, Reid holds that we are so constituted
that we have certain innate dispositions to belief, which are activated by common experience, particularly by sensation, and yield
beliefs that everyone has, cannot help having, and are (perhaps
for that reason) justified. These are the commonsense beliefs of
which Reid and his followers are taken by everyone to be the de-
fenders. On Wolterstorff's account, these beliefs do not include
theistic beliefs; for Reid follows the standard Enlightenment practice of maintaining that these depend for their justification on
the work of natural theology, particularly the Design Argument.
What Wolterstorff's conclusion suggests is that we are now in a
position to see that Reid's rebuttal of Humean skepticism regarding our beliefs in the external world, the regularity of nature, and
personal identity is a rebuttal that could have been extended, and
should have been extended, to theistic beliefs as well. When this
extension is made (and I speculate a little here), we enter an epistemological world in which the reading of Scripture, or perhaps
other forms of religious experience, can be seen to function in
relation to theistic beliefs in the way in which sense-experience
functions in relation to beliefs about the external world: as the
occasion of generally justified beliefs. I take this to be a proclama-
tion of the apologetic position I have been outlining, prompted
by the examination of a philosopher who is seen as having come
three-quarters of the way toward it, but to have been held back
by the limitations of Enlightenment foundationalism.

I would like to approach this historically. Reid was responding to Hume. How did Hume view Reid's response? A common view is that he did not respond at all, either because he could not or because he thought he need not. David Norton has shown, I think, that this is not correct.[5] I agree that it is not but will state my own view on the details, which is not the same as Norton's, because I read Hume slightly differently.[6]

Hume holds, as I read him, that the skeptic is right in maintaining that philosophy cannot supply us with rational justifications for our basic beliefs about our environment and ourselves. Suspense of judgment about these matters, however, is not a psychological option for us, except for very brief periods in the study. Nature has so constituted us that we have a number of beliefs of fundamental importance to human life, despite the fact that rational justification of them is unavailable. This dispensation of nature is fortunate for us and can be augmented for good by active participation in society and by the avoidance of overindulgence in philosophical questioning and of the misguided pursuit of the "monkish virtues" of private religion.

This Darwinian view of our natural beliefs has important affinities with Reid's position, since both Hume and Reid say that belief is natural for us, and that skepticism is correspondingly a closed option. But there is an important difference also. Reid appears to think that the beliefs are not merely ineluctable but are somehow shown by this to be true—a position mirrored in the twentieth century by G. E. Moore in his "Defence of Common Sense." Hume clearly does not hold this; and, as Norton makes clear, the difference between them is due to the fact that when Reid ascribes belief-propensities to our nature, he sees this nature as providentially structured by God. This is perhaps why he does not treat theism as arising from this nature itself but as justifiable independently. Hume, on the other hand, spends much of his intellectual powers undermining this theistic understanding of human nature and substituting a purely secular account. As a consequence, Hume always avoids any claim that the natural beliefs are true, or at least that we can claim to know that they are. In this respect he is at one with classical Pyrrhonism; he only departs from it in his insistence that we are not at liberty to withhold belief when we despair of finding justification.[7] Hence Hume did not contest Reid's view that we are so constituted that we will assent to the basic propositions of common sense, because he agreed with it; but he did answer Reid's conviction that the canon of common sense consisted of true propositions by undermining the providential theism on which this view depended.

A position like the one I have found in Wolterstorff amounts to an extension of Reid's position on commonsense beliefs to include theistic beliefs: They are now to be seen as occasioned by religious experience, or by the reading of Scripture, in the way in which beliefs about our environment are occasioned by sensory experience. Just as the absence of independent philosophical foundations for common sense does not, in Reid's view, matter, so the absence of independent justification for theism in natural theology does not, in Wolterstorff's view, matter either.

There is, however, one obvious problem. The theistic beliefs that are now included among those commitments exempted from the demand for independent justification have competitors in a way that commonsense beliefs do not appear to have. There are, to put it conservatively, a number of apparently competing religious worldviews, each claiming to express the perception of our universe that is natural to us, and each occasioned, for those who come to share it, by some easily accessible experience or phenomenon. Hence there is little temptation for those who use this mode of apologetic to claim that such experiences activate instant knowledge. Wolterstorff speaks instead of justified beliefs. In a much more fully developed version of this apologetic, William Alston, sensitive to the competing belief-claims of alternative religious traditions, says that religious experience gives prima facie justification, rather than ultimate justification, for the beliefs it occasions. Alvin Plantinga appears to accept that theistic beliefs occasioned by religious experience are only justified if there are no potential "defeaters" (such as the problem of evil) that undermine them. At the heart of each version of this view, however, is an insistence that just as (it is said) commonsense beliefs have no need of independent philosophical support in addition to the sensory experiences that occasion them, so theistic beliefs have no need of independent philosophical support in addition to the experiences that occasion them: that to demand such support in the theological case, while not demanding it in the sensory case, is to be guilty of epistemic chauvinism.

I think that Hume tried to head off this sort of argument, even though it had not been explicitly formulated in this antifoundational form. For he does not only attack, and destroy, the Design Argument on which Reid and his predecessors leaned so heavily. His writings on religion also contain arguments intended to undermine the analogy between commonsense beliefs and belief in God. For example, the *Natural History of Religion* tells us that, unlike our natural beliefs, religious beliefs are not universal; it also tells us that the sources of religious beliefs are not natural, but environmental and cultural. The intent (as I read it) of part 12 of the *Dialogues Concerning Natural Religion* is in part to show that even if impulses to theism are not undermined by the failure of the Design Argument, they cannot extend to the acceptance of the moral goodness of God or the need for private devotions.

Whether Hume is successful or not, he seems to me to be aware, as Reid apparently was not, that the recognition of the naturalness of commonsense belief opened a possible line of religious apologetic that he was very anxious to resist. I speculate further: Hume's awareness of this form of apologetic is the result of his having encountered it—not in Reid, who, as we have seen, does not use it or even seem to see its possibility—but in someone from whom I feel sure he had learned, namely, Pascal.[8]

III.

On the surface, no two thinkers could be more different from one another than Pascal and Hume. Certainly their objectives are exactly opposed, each adopting commitments that the other passionately rejects. But there are instructive parallels too, and their attitudes to the Pyrrhonian tradition bring these out most clearly. Both would agree that skepticism exposes the emptiness of rationalist philosophical systems. Both would also agree that this emptiness extends to the realm of natural, or philosophical, theology. Both find the Pyrrhonian suspense of judgment a practical impossibility. Each finds the skeptic's omnivorous doubts and questions deeply disturbing and sees Pyrrhonism, therefore, as leading to anxiety and despair, not tranquillity. And each finds instinctive resources in human nature that protect us from that anxiety by committing us to beliefs that make human life possible. They divide, however, at this point. One minor difference is that Pascal is prepared to say that these beliefs, in secular cases, constitute knowledge, whereas Hume speaks only of natural *beliefs*. The major difference is that Pascal urges us to conquer the wretchedness we find in the human life we enter by opening ourselves to faith; but Hume, thinking that faith, too, is another, needless source of anxiety and distress, holds that only if we confine ourselves to secular concerns can peace of mind be a real possibility for us.

But Hume sees that this last step opens him to possible charges of inconsistency. On what grounds can he welcome the commitments that common sense represents, yet stop short of yielding to the claims of faith, when they, too, fill in the gap that the Pyrrhonist has opened? I suggest that many of the arguments I have referred to above are designed by Hume to deal with this problem.

If I am right that Hume perceived this problem in response to Pascal, whose diagnosis he largely accepted but whose prescriptions repelled him, then I think it is also instructive to notice that Pascal, and Hume himself, develop their views (including their negative views on natural theology) in response to skepticism. Both seem to have learned about skepticism at second hand, through Montaigne, and (in Hume's case) through Pierre Bayle. And skepticism to them was not the fabricated and anonymous skepticism of Descartes's *Meditations*, but the real, live, Hellenistic variety presented by Sextus Empiricus. They think that nature supplies us with an antidote to skeptic arguments, but not an answer. The antidote comes from the fact that it has made us incapable of adopting, or at least incapable of sustaining, the suspense of judgment through which the Pyrrhonist claimed to find tranquillity. They also think that those short periods during which skepticial uncertainty can take hold of us are enough to show that it could never yield tranquillity in any case, but only be itself a source of anxiety and despair. When Hume tells us that belief is "more properly an act of the sensitive, than of the cogitative part of our natures,"[9] he is echoing Pascal's doctrine of the heart.[10] He differs from him in two key ways. First, his view of convention and social engagement is positive and benign: It reinforces nature by involving us in activities for which we are fitted, and by fending off the anxieties that come from immoderate indulgence in philosophical questioning. Second, he rejects the claims of popular religion, since these generate independent forms of anxiety and impose unnatural moral demands that hinder us from exercising our natural talents for social life. To Pascal, on the other hand, most social convention is a conspiracy to prevent the heart from turning to God, who has made himself available to us in the person of Christ and the sacraments of his church. This conspiracy blocks the only real solution to despair and anxiety, namely, faith, which is the extension to God and his revelation of the natural assent that the heart also gives to the claims of science and common sense that the skeptic has questioned.

Hume's hostility to popular religion does not extend to "philosophical" religion. Insofar as we can take what he says in part 12 of the *Dialogues* at face value, Hume, speaking through Philo, seems willing enough to accommodate himself to the polite conventional, quasi-deistic religion to which he reduces the doctrines of Cleanthes in that work, and which he saw around him in the persons and practices of his friends among the Scottish Moderates. Such religion is a part of the social cement that holds polite society together, and has to be distinguished from the superstitious and enthusiastic variety represented in the *Dialogues* by

Demea. In taking this view, at least in public, Hume is treating religion (or what he disingenuously refers to as true religion) in a manner strongly reminiscent of Sextus Empiricus, who says: "Although, following the ordinary view, we affirm undogmatically that Gods exist and reverence Gods and ascribe to them foreknowledge, yet as against the rashness of the Dogmatists we argue as follows." [11] The classical skeptic accommodates himself undogmatically, or beliefflessly, to the conventional pieties but turns aside from the dogmatic controversies about the gods' ultimate reality or nature. Although the extent of Hume's direct acquaintance with Sextus is unclear, his position on religion seems to me to have been close to the beliefless conformity Sextus expresses (and which Montaigne, to Pascal's anger, imitated).

IV.

What does this historical detour show us? Let me first rehearse the various estimates of religious belief and commonsense belief that I have mentioned.

First, there is classical Pyrrhonism as we find it in Sextus. The stance of the Pyrrhonist on both secular and religious opinion is the same. As a member of a particular society, he sees his world, including its deities, as his time and place disposes him to see them. He reads all the philosophical arguments about these opinions, or appearances as he calls them, and finds himself sated by arguments that say they correspond to realities, and arguments that say they do not. He finds himself suspending judgment on whether they do or do not correspond to realities, and retains an open mind on this; but in finding himself in this state, he is able to be at ease with himself by participating in his world without the concern his fellows have for determining whether their opinions have some kind of cosmic warrant. His life is not unexamined, but he no longer seeks for meaning in it. He conforms beliefflessly.

Next, there is Pascal. Pyrrhonism, he says, is true:[12] Philosophy cannot carry us from appearances to reality. But we will not find tranquillity by shrugging our shoulders in the face of this. Nor will we find it by seeking distraction in society and play; these merely conceal the anxieties of fear and meaninglessness with which the impotence of reason confronts us. We are so endowed by Providence, however, that we can bypass doubts about our commonsense world through the dictates of the heart. If we turn to divine grace, and open our heart to God, faith will then give us the certitude and the meaning that the Pyrrhonists have shown reason cannot supply. Just as Descartes's proofs of the external world are unnecessary, so attending to his proofs of God merely postpones the leap of faith that will lead to peace.

Then there is Hume. Again, reason cannot supply us with knowledge of the external world, the regularity of nature, or the stability of the self; but human nature supplies us with the belief in these things that enables us to function in the world whose inner nature reason cannot penetrate. Without this, we would be victims of paralysis, indecision, and anxiety. Nature also provides us with social proclivities, so that we can reinforce those natural beliefs and keep philosophical anxieties at bay by indulging in the very society and play that Pascal rejected. The major threat to social harmony and individual peace of mind is the very religion that Pascal sought to lead us into. Reason can come to our aid here, however, by showing that belief in God is not rooted in our natures and cannot be supported by scientific argument. Reason can also come to our aid by stripping popular religion of its disturbing doctrines and enthusiasms, and by fabricating a formal and domesticated piety that reinforces social conformity, much as the classical Pyrrhonist continued to reverence the deities of his day.

Next, we have Reid: He tells essentially the same story as Hume about the place of commonsense beliefs in our natures but supposes he is refuting the skepticism of Hume by calling the natural beliefs forms of knowledge. Any justification for this dogmatic move comes from his view that the nature with which we are endowed has been given us by God; this claim, however, seems to depend in his system on the very Design Argument that Hume refuted in the *Dialogues*.

In our own time we have Wolterstorff and others who argue that Reid should have been more careful and insisted merely on the claim that our commonsense beliefs are justified by our encounter with the appearances that occasion them; and that he should have said the same thing about theistic beliefs, instead of resorting to natural theology to justify them. For the experiences that give rise to theistic beliefs stand in the same relationship to them as the experiences that occasion our commonsense beliefs about our environment stand to those commonsense beliefs. Since the latter are rational, the former are too.

In all these complex positions, is there any position held by everyone? It seems that there is one, and only one: that the natural beliefs of common sense are held in the absence of independent reasoned justification. From this only the classical Pyrrhonist infers that we can get along without them. No one else believes him, and all insist that our nature predetermines we will accept them. They disagree on how rational this makes these commonsense beliefs, with Pascal and Hume telling us, in different tones of voice, that they are due to a power in us that is distinct from reason, and Reid and Wolterstorff saying that it is indeed rational to adopt them. All except Reid hold that the efforts of natural theology to provide independent rational grounds for religious beliefs are misguided, but they divide very sharply on the implications of this. To Sextus and Hume, it means that the "man of letters," as Hume describes him, will be immunized against all forms of religion that require belief, but need not resist those conformist rituals that do not. To Pascal and to Wolterstorff, faith does not need the proffered justification of the natural theologian, and the rationality of faith is exactly analogous to that of the beliefs of common sense, needing as little apology as they do. Reid alone stands out as holding back from the simple equation of the epistemic status of commonsense beliefs and theistic beliefs.

I want to argue that he was both philosophically and theologically wise to hesitate. To bring this out, I shall make two more statements of a historical sort.

V.

The first statement is probably uncontroversial. It is that in recent religious thought there has been an increasing concern with the fact that the truth-claims of a particular religion, such as Christianity, compete for our acceptance with those of other religious traditions. While this has always been true, it has been easy enough in the past to ignore it. So debate about the claims of Christianity has commonly been carried on as though the range of what William James calls open options is confined to the various versions of Christianity on the one side, and the more austere charms of atheism or agnosticism on the other. Philosophy of religion still proceeds, quite often, in this way. But issues of religious epistemology are grossly oversimplified by this. One sign of the increasing awareness of this fact is the anxiety with which some scholars have argued that the apparent incompatibilities between the major religious traditions of the world are only superficial. In what follows I shall not argue against that judgment, but I shall assume that it needs more justification than it has so far been given by anyone.

The fact of religious pluralism was recognized long ago by Sextus and his skeptic colleagues, who used it to support relativistic conformism. But the views of thinkers such as Wolterstorff, Alston, and Plantinga face a serious problem when the facts of religious pluralism are recognized. For if one maintains that some key religious beliefs of one's own tradition can be held without inference from independent foundations or are properly basic, one has to confront the fact that a parallel case can readily be made for key beliefs of other, incompatible religious traditions. If one supplements one's claim for the proper basicality of one's beliefs by saying they are occasioned by religious experiences, a parallel point can be made for the indigenous experiences of the other traditions also. In accepting the beliefs of one tradition, one may find oneself forced to deny those of another and, by implication, judging the experiences that occasion them to be religiously inauthentic. A parallel with the commonsense beliefs of perception is enough, in my view, to show that the believer in a tradition is *rational* or justified prima facie in assenting on the basis of his or her experiences; but this is not apologetically sufficient to justify *sustaining* that assent in the face of the contrasting claims of incompatible traditions. There is parity between commonsense beliefs and religious ones, but for religion, parity is not enough. If we content ourselves with the recognition that it is rational to hold our religious commitments (if we have them) as basic beliefs, we have to face living in a religiously Balkanized world. It is not clear to me that one can acquiesce in this Balkanization without relapsing into some form of the relativist conformism of the classical skeptic. This is not a garden path down which a person of faith can afford to wander.

I have expressed this elsewhere by saying that our world exhibits *multiple religious ambiguity*. So far, I have taken this to be an ambiguity that obtains between one religion and others. But it can also obtain between secular systems of thought, such as Marxism, Freudianism, and sociobiology; for these can have their own apparently revelatory experiences and illuminations, their own all-embracing claims about human nature and its hidden defects and opportunities, and their own built-in devices for explaining away the claims of one another. And there is the ambiguity that the world wears between any given one of these religious or nonreligious systems, and the unsystematic commonsense world of the unexamined life, which also has its indigenous illuminations in the form of the existentialist's sense of the absurd or the comforting reassurance Hume was able to arrange for himself at the backgammon table.

In this situation, it seems to me that the wise apologist for religion should take the position that Reid takes, and not the position that Pascal or Wolterstorff or Alston prefers. For he is the only one who has an answer to the threat posed by the fact of ambiguity. The threat is, once more, that although it is rational to yield to the claims of those religious beliefs that are occasioned by the religious experiences one may have, it is also rational for those who have experiences that occasion incompatible religious beliefs to accept them, and for those whose experiences are intrinsically secularizing ones to reject religion altogether. Reid's answer is consistent with Hume's claim that although the beliefs of common sense are universal, the beliefs of religion are not. It is the resort to natural theology.

When I say Reid has an answer, I do not mean that there is much in Reid in the way of natural theology.[13] I mean merely that Reid shows wisdom in not rejecting the claims of natural theology when his doctrine of common sense might have tempted him to do so. In this he shows, I think, an awareness of what natural theology was all about that contemporary basic believers do not show. They seem to suppose that to engage in natural theology is to commit oneself to the view that without it, religious belief is irrational. They are right to hold that religious belief does not need independent rational support from natural theology to be rational. But the classic natural theologians were not just arguing for the rationality of believing in the existence of God or the providential governance of the world. They were trying to show that it was *ir*rational *not* to believe in these things. That is what we mean when we say they were trying to prove them.

If someone were to succeed in proving them, he or she would achieve something of very great epistemic importance. For such a proof would disambiguate our world. At least, it would do so for all those who begin with the premises of the proofs. If these premises are premises of secular common sense, then a successful demonstration in natural theology would show that it is irrational for someone who accepts them not to be a theist also.

I suggested earlier that such an achievement would have religious value. Let me indicate briefly why I think this, since many believers follow Pascal and Kierkegaard in denying it. It is a significant tenet of many theologians that unbelief is not mere error but is blameworthy: that those who do not believe in God reject him for morally bad motives and deceive themselves. Now even if this is true in many cases, it is most unlikely to be true in all cases, *if* we live in a religiously ambiguous world. For the very ambiguity of the world is itself a plausible reason for withholding belief. If the world were disambiguated by the production of a demonstration, then it might be true that those who knew about it could then only disbelieve for morally discreditable reasons. But not otherwise. If this is right, then I see the lack of cogent proofs of God as a problem for theology, not something theologians should welcome or even be resigned to. They should immediately set about rectifying it. Some of them have, as I said at the outset. But their heart is not really in it, because they overvalue the Basic Belief Apologetic.

To summarize: I agree that the arguments of Wolterstorff, Alston, and Plantinga succeed in their objective of showing that it is rational to hold religious beliefs without the independent support of natural theology. But this does not provide the basis of a satisfactory response to the problems attendant on religious pluralism and ambiguity and makes it more difficult to ascribe unbelief to sinfulness. In these respects, at least, it does not represent an advance on the purer fideism of Pascal or Kierkegaard.[14] I shall now try to answer some actual and possible objections to my argument.

VI.

I begin with the status of the claim that unbelief is due to sin. The Christian understanding of human nature is preeminent, though not unique, in helping us understand the extent to which beliefs we like to think of as due entirely to the disinterested consideration of the facts are instead the result of selfish motives. We believe things because it suits us to believe them, and we disbelieve things because it does not suit us to acknowledge them. Nothing I have said is intended to undermine the recognition of this. If one recognizes it, however, one should also recognize that we have the power to believe things that have been proved false to us and to disbelieve things that have been proved to us to be true. Philosophers have more training than most to do these things, but all of us can manage them. We also have the power, of course, to recognize that something is proved or disproved to us, yet never act on this recognition. These facts have to be accommodated, I think, in any attempt to define what a proof is or what criteria must be satisfied when one is attempted. If this is true, then a likely example of unbelief being due to sin would be someone's not believing in God when God's existence had been proved to him.[15] More to the present purpose, if an unbeliever has *not* had God's existence proved to him, then even though his doubts about God may still be sinful ones, there is less reason to suppose them to be. That person's world will quite rationally be judged by him to be religiously ambiguous or to yield potential defeaters of religious claims to which he does not have a sound answer. Minimally, and with the fullest allowance for human corruption and self-deceit, a religiously ambiguous world is one in which unbelievers have good excuses for their doubts, even if their doubts are not conscientious ones. An excuse can be a good one, even if the person who offers it has tainted motives for doing so. But whenever a good excuse is available, the judgment that such a person's motives are tainted is less plausible.

In our own day, as I have argued earlier, those who live in societies in which Christianity has been the dominant faith are confronted by the claims of other faiths and the claims of secular worldviews that compete with these faiths and with one another. Many in these cultures grow to maturity without serious exposure to the claims of Christianity, which then confronts them as one of a wide range of personal options. While no one can see into the breast of another, I venture the suggestion that in this situation, in which an enquirer may have absorbed some of the predispositions of non-Christian faiths or have been exposed hitherto to purely secular understandings of the world, conscientious doubts about Christian claims are not merely likely to occur but may well last a lifetime. I would also venture the suggestion that denying this possibility is not merely unrealistic but uncharitable.

It is true, of course, that the world in which multiple religious ambiguity obtains is a world in which each of us inherits many centuries of cultural development. Even if a given person is confronted with a range of religious and secular choices without having a predisposition to make a Christian choice, and he lacks this predisposition through no fault of his own, the culture he inherits has developed in the way it has because of a multitude of choices by his forebears—choices that have progressively robbed us of the natural inclination to experience our world in a Christian fashion, so that Christian interpretations of it are increasingly seen as wholly optional additions to a common fund of secular understandings. These cultural choices may well be judged to be corrupted by sin, however the mind-set of the individual himself is assessed. The Christian tradition has always insisted on the reality of collective responsibility in one way or another. I assume, however, that the claim that it is sinfulness that prevents us from believing is a claim that ascribes to each individual an essential core of guilt for not transcending the hindrances that the cultural environment introduces.[16] And I suggest that the success of some form of natural theology would give those able to understand it a clear means of transcending those hindrances, if they chose to do so. If they did not so choose, their individual responsibility for continued unbelief would be less questionable.

VII.

I have argued so far that if no body of successful natural theology were available, it could still be true that unbelief is always sinful or blameworthy because our epistemic attitudes are easily corrupted. But its likelihood would be less than it would be if a successful body of natural theology *were* available.

I need to say more, however, about how success in the enterprise of natural theology would change our epistemic situation, especially since I have agreed that successful natural theology could be disregarded. What, exactly, is parity not enough *for*?

I shall take it that a natural theologian is in the business of providing proofs. As I am using this term, a proof of something is relative to a particular hearer or reader and is only successful if that hearer's epistemic situation is addressed. It is successful if it makes it clear to a hearer who knows the truth of the argument's premises, that they entail, or make it overwhelmingly probable, that God exists or that some proposition that entails his existence is true. Since natural theologians normally wish to reach a large audience, they usually begin with premises that they think almost everybody knows, but I do not see this to be necessary. It is also unnecessary, I think, for the premises to be metaphysical in nature or to be of a very general observational character. They could well be historical or be reports of events known of, or experienced by, the hearer. This would open the range of possible proofs to include arguments based on alleged miracles, for example, and would include among them items traditionally classified as evidences or as preambles to faith.

Suppose some such argument is successful, so that someone has had God's existence proved to him or to her. I have already said that people can manage to go on disbelieving something that has been proved to them. We have many devices available for this. When we see the unwelcome conclusion coming, we can persist in questioning the inference from the premises we have accepted; or we can question those premises themselves, if necessary, by undermining our own previous knowledge of them; or we can drive the conclusion out of our heads by associating exclusively with people who are sure it is false. A successful piece of natural theology could be countered in all these ways. So it might not create any converts. But it would take away a good excuse for unbelief. It would do this by providing an opportunity to transcend the cultural hindrances presented by the religious ambiguity and secularity of our world.

To expand further, I can best make it clear by concentrating on an important feature of the Basic Belief Apologetic that I have hitherto passed over too quickly. The power of that apologetic does not, as I mistakenly supposed when I first encountered it, depend entirely on the negative similarity between basic commonsense beliefs and basic religious beliefs. It is not just a matter of noting that the former are not inferred from other beliefs any more than the latter are. It also depends on the fact that both sorts of beliefs are occasioned by (or are "grounded" in) certain experiences that the believing subject has. This enables Plantinga, for example, to emphasize that religious beliefs are not rendered groundless because they are basic; and Alston, especially, stresses that believers are sustained in their faith by the experiences they claim to have of God's presence or love or forgiveness. Now in a religiously ambiguous world, it is possible for many to be hindered from having such experiences by the secularism of our culture or by its religious pluralism; and it is possible also to *have* such experiences without being sure, at all, whether to accept that they *are* experiences of God's presence as they seem to be, for alternative understandings of them immediately suggest themselves to the subject having them, as well as to others judging the subject's situation from without.

It is not hard to see a role for natural theology in a world like this. It is a role that should be fully acceptable to those who insist that belief in God is rational without natural theology and that it requires grounding in direct experience of his presence. The role is that of removing the cultural hindrances to the occurrence of such experience or to the recognition of their meaning. It is the role of providing an antidote to the potential defeaters of claims grounded in such experience. It is the role of creating, or facilitating, an openness to such experience or even a rational expectation of it. Natural theology would fulfill this role because of the disambiguating function it would perform.

There is an objection to all this. Why am I so sure that a proof of God would disambiguate our world? Could it not be rationally and conscientiously resisted? Believers often say they do not have a clear answer to such deep theological difficulties as the problem of evil or the paradox of grace and freedom; but they continue believing by saying these difficulties must have a solution, even though they do not expect to uncover it. Argument is needed to show this is irrational or corrupt, to say the least, though doubtless it does involve a conflict of beliefs. Could the same not be true in reverse? Could not a secularist, or the adherent of a faith inconsistent with Christian theism, react to a proof in natural theology the same way, saying there has to be a catch in it somewhere?

To reply, I must point to a feature of natural theology I have not emphasized enough before. It is called *natural* theology not because its premises are known to everyone, but because they can be known to be true without already knowing or believing that God exists and without any grounding in experience of God. This externality has made some judge natural theology to be an attempt to provide foundations for religious belief when they are not needed. But this same externality would free a successful exercise of natural theology from the limitations imposed on other religious claims by the multiple religious ambiguity of our world, for it would begin from premises that required no concession to the worldview of the theist; yet acceptance of its conclusion would entail that very worldview. An argument that would be so clearly disambiguating if it were successful would have an epistemic importance that would make it self-evidently irresponsible to put it on one side. It would be intellectually obligatory for those who found its conclusion unwelcome (and probably for some of those who did not) to examine it and be sure it was not flawed.

I have not argued here that there *is* any successful natural theology. I have merely argued that in our multiply ambiguous world, natural theology would have a function quite distinct from the dubious functions of providing foundations for religious beliefs or bypassing the need for religious experience. If this function cannot be discharged because there is no successful natural theology to be had, then I think that the Christian has a theological problem: Why is our world ambiguous? I cannot tell how far *this* is a difficulty that can responsibly be put on one side.

Notes

Acknowledgment: An earlier version of this essay was read at a conference sponsored by Simon Fraser University, British Columbia, in February 1987. I am grateful for the comments on that version that were presented by David Copp, though I do not think he would agree with what I say here.

1. See Norman Malcolm, "Anselm's Ontological Arguments," *The Philosophical Review* 99 (1960); Alvin Plantinga, *The Nature of Necessity* (Oxford: Oxford University Press, 1974); Clement Dore, *Theism* (Dordrecht: Reidel, 1984).

2. R. G. Swinburne, *The Existence of God* (Oxford: Oxford University Press, 1979); Hugo Meynell, *The Intelligible Universe* (London: Macmillan, 1982).

3. See the essays by Alvin Plantinga, William Alston, and Nicholas Wolterstorff in *Faith and Rationality*, ed. Alvin Plantinga and Nicholas Wolterstorff (Notre Dame: University of Notre Dame Press, 1983); Alvin Plantinga, "Is Belief in God Rational?" in *Rationality and Religious Belief*, ed. C. F. Delaney (Notre Dame: University of Notre Dame Press, 1979); and William Alston, "Perceiving God," *Journal of Philosophy* 83 (1986).

4. Nicholas Wolterstorff, "Thomas Reid on Rationality," in *Rationality in the Calvinian Tradition*, ed. H. Hart and J. van der Hoeven (Washington, D.C.: University Press of America, 1983), p. 67.

5. David Fate Norton, *David Hume: Common-Sense Moralist, Sceptical Metaphysician* (Princeton: Princeton University Press, 1982), chap. 5.

6. Terence Penelhum, *Hume* (New York: St. Martin's Press, 1975); and idem, "Hume's Skepticism and the Dialogues" in *McGill Hume Studies*, ed. David Fate Norton, Nicholas Capaldi, and Wade L. Robison (Austin Hill Press, 1979).

7. For the extent to which Hume remains skeptical despite his doctrine of natural belief, see John P. Wright, *The Sceptical Realism of David Hume* (Manchester: Manchester University Press, 1983).

8. What follows is developed more fully in Terence Penelhum, *God and Skepticism* (Dordrecht: Reidel, 1983), esp. chaps. 4, 6.

9. David Hume, *Treatise of Human Nature*, ed. L. A. Selby-Bigge (Oxford: Oxford University Press, 1888), p. 183.

10. Pascal, *Pensées*, Fragment 423 (Lafuma) 277 (Brunschvicg).

11. Sextus Empiricus, *Outlines of Pyrrhonism*, 3, 2, 327, vol. 1 of the Loeb edition of Sextus, trans. R. G. Bury.

12. Pascal, *Pensées* 691–432.

13. We now have available a volume of Thomas Reid's *Lectures on Natural Theology*, ed. Elmer H. Duncan (Washington, D.C.: University Press of America, 1981). The text is based on student notes of the lectures delivered in 1780; the lectures were not published by Reid himself. In large part they consist of presentations of the Design Argument for the existence of God, which Reid sees as a first stage in the rational testing of the claims of the Christian revelation. I find them lacking in the acuity and vigor of Reid's better-known works. It has been suggested that Reid's own cultural and historical setting led him to accept the standard natural theology of the time "by default rather than reasoned historical conviction." If this were true, what I have credited to his wisdom may be due to inertia. See Stewart R. Sutherland, "The Presbyterian Inheritance of Hume and Reid" in *The Origins and Nature of the Scottish Enlightenment*, ed. R. H. Campbell and A. S. Skinner (Edinburgh: J. Donald, 1982) pp. 131–49.

14. The term "fideism" needs more clarification than it usually receives, and I plead guilty to sinning here. For a start, see Plantinga's remarks near the close of his essay in *Faith and Rationality*.

15. Unfortunately these obvious truths are overlooked very frequently. I have before me a typical example from a British Sunday newspaper. "Since belief cannot be proven, there has to be a choice of whether to believe or not. If God's existence were undoubtable we should all have to become His abject slaves and there could be no exchange of love between us and Him, no point in being human." Gerald Priestland, "Thank God for the Essential Atheist," *Sunday Times*, 5 March 1989.

16. I am trying here to answer some of the criticisms of my arguments in R. J. Feenstra's essay "Natural Theology, Epistemic Parity, and Unbelief," *Modern Theology* 5 (1988).

Richard H. Popkin

4

FIDEISM, QUIETISM, AND UNBELIEF: SKEPTICISM FOR AND AGAINST RELIGION IN THE SEVENTEENTH AND EIGHTEENTH CENTURIES

In the forty years that I have been researching and writing on the history of skepticism, I have been interested in the role that skepticism and skeptical arguments have played as a purported basis for religious belief from the time of Erasmus and Montaigne and the Counter-Reformers to Kierkegaard and the Russian Orthodox theologians of the twentieth century. I have had a growing interest during the last twenty years or so in the way skepticism and skeptical arguments have been applied to religious issues by seventeenth-century Bible scholars, religious reformers, deists, and nonbelievers to create modern irreligion from the time of Spinoza through the French and English enlightenments. This application became the basis of the critical deism of Tom Paine and the atheism of Robert Ingersol and Bertrand Russell.

I have also been exploring for the last decade or so the use of skeptical weapons by Jews against Christians and Christians against Jews in the seventeenth-century, and the way this prepared the way for the rejection of both religions by Voltaire and Baron d'Holbach in the French Enlightenment.

I should like now to explore some of the issues that were involved, some of the anticipated results by the parties involved, and some of the ways the skeptical materials became transformed from an alleged defense of religion to a way of casting grave or complete doubt upon it.

Although my essay will be cast as a historical narrative and an examination of historically presented positions, I hope, as Kierkegaard might say, that it has more than historical import, though it takes off from a historical point of departure. For better or worse, I am a historian of intellectual activity and can best deal with questions when I approach them in the historical context in which they arose. I shall briefly indicate the role of modern fideism and of modern quietism as defenses of religion. Then I shall look at the irreligious possibilities that opponents then and now have seen in these outlooks and at some of the irreligious developments that occurred, especially from Spinoza onward. Finally I shall attempt to assess the positive and negative roles that skepticism and skeptical arguments have played in modern religious history.

Since I am not an analytic philosopher, I shall have to leave it to my colleagues in this volume to clarify and examine some of these issues and to assess whether "reasonable people" should have come to the conclusions that some of our intellectual ancestors did.

As I tried to show in my *History of Scepticism* and in many articles about Pascal, Hume, and Kierkegaard, ancient skeptical arguments that appeared in Sextus Empiricus, Cicero, and Diogenes Laertius were rediscovered in the sixteenth century and were immediately employed in the religious controversies of the time, principally by Catholic arguers.[1] Starting with Erasmus in his controversy with Martin Luther, the attempt was made by using skeptical arguments to show that the Reformers had insufficient evidence to support their claims, and that *per non sequitur,* one should remain a Catholic by faith alone.[2] Montaigne and his disciple Father Pierre Charron developed a Christian Pyrrhonism. They first present arguments from Sextus and Cicero to undermine confidence in our sensory and rational faculties, our judgments, and our sensory evidence. This, they suggest, should lead one to suspend judgment, to blank out the contents of one's mind, ready to accept whatever God pleases to reveal to us. And whatever this is, we should accept on faith.[3]

Montaigne briefly indicates that his skepticism undermines any reason for becoming a Protestant.[4] (Montaigne's mother, who was of Jewish ancestry, became one of the first Protestants in France. Montaigne lived with his mother and was obviously somewhat terrified by his Catholic father, who died before Montaigne wrote his *Essais*. There may be a good Freudian explanation of Montaigne's nonrational rejection of Protestantism.) The editor of the first complete Latin edition of Sextus Empiricus in 1569, Gentian Hervet, the secretary of the Cardinal of Lorraine, tells us that he translated and edited Sextus for relaxation after participating in the Council of Trent. He then said that Sextus provided the perfect answer to Calvinism. If nothing can be known, then Calvinism cannot be known![5] Montaigne's cousin Francisco Sanches, in the best philosophical presentation of skepticism of the time, his *Quod Nihil Scitur* of 1576 (which has just been published in English translation for the first time), spends almost all of his text arguing that Aristotelian knowledge is unattainable as is Platonic knowledge. So, as the title says, *nihil scitur*. In a closing line, Sanches argues one should accept Christianity on faith.[6] Some have suggested that he was not a Christian but was a secret Jew, like his ancestors, and he just threw in the fideistic closing lines to make the authorities happy.

People of the time suspected Montaigne and Sanches of insincerity.[7] I have been exploring the belief world of the Marranos, the forced converts to Christianity in Spain and Portugal, and their descendents, who moved into the Marrano Diaspora in southern France, Italy, Amsterdam, and elsewhere. There is ample reason to suspect that many of them were not sincere Christians or even Christians at all. But each case has to be judged on its merits and evidence. And I do not think we have enough information about the actual beliefs and practices of either Montaigne or Sanches to ascertain what they did believe beyond what is on the printed page.

The fideistic view was presented at length by Montaigne's disciple Father Pierre Charron, a noted theologian of the time and the protegé of a minor French bishop. His first work is a huge opus, *Les Trois Véritez*, in which he contends against atheists that God exists (the first truth), against Jews, Turks, and others, that Christianity is the true religion (the second truth), and against Protestants that Catholicism is the true form of Christianity (the third truth). Each truth is "established" by skeptical arguments against atheists, Jews, Turks, and Protestants, showing that they have no evidential basis for holding their views.[8] This skeptical defense of Catholicism was followed by Charron's most famous work, *De la Sagesse* (On wisdom). Here, Charron sets forth Montaigne's rambling views in didactic fashion, first developing the basis for complete suspension of judgment, then claiming that one should accept religion on faith and should live according to a natural morality.[9] The position of Montaigne and Charron was supported by many important figures in French Catholicism, and in one form or another it became a dominant "defense" of Catholicism in France during the Counter-Reformation.[10] One French thinker said that this skeptical view was based on the teachings of *"le divin Sexte"* (the divine Sextus), the author of "notre Décalogue."[11]

By and large, the followers of Montaigne, who were significant figures through the ages of Louis XIII and Louis XIV, showed no particular fervor in their religious views or practices and, with the exception of Charron, produced no religious writings. Their fideistic Catholicism seems quite tepid, if sincere. Their contemporary, Blaise Pascal, who developed the strongest statement of their case in the seventeenth century, felt that Montaigne's view, in fact, represented "the misery of man without God."[12] Pascal, using the skepticism of Montaigne and the hyperbolic doubt introduced by Descartes, intensified the skeptical case and made being overwhelmed by it the prelude to reaching religious faith.

Since no one who is not perverse can doubt Pascal's religious sincerity, I shall take his (and Kierkegaard's) formulation of fideism as the central statements of the position. As is well known, Pascal, after becoming one of the foremost mathematicians and physicists of his time, had an overpowering religious experience, retired to the monastery at Port-Royal and worked on an apology for the Christian religion. The *Pensées*, fragments written on slips of paper, were found in his room when he died and seem to be this apology, albeit unfinished.[13]

In one central *pensée* (131–434), Pascal begins by developing a skepticism beyond that of Descartes's First Meditation. "We have no certainty of the truth of these principles [the basic truths upon which all other knowledge claims rest] *apart from faith and revelation*, except in so far as we naturally perceive them in ourselves." Natural intuition "is not a convincing proof of their truth; since, having no certainty, *apart from faith*, whether man was created by a good God, or by a wicked demon, or by chance, it is doubtful whether these principles given us are true, or false or uncertain, according to our origin" (my emphasis).[14] So, the certainty of our knowledge depends on who or what produced us with our faculties. It does no good to appeal to Descartes's God, who cannot deceive, since the value of the appeal, apart from faith or revelation, again depends on our origin. As Pascal pursues the skeptical implications, as well as the natural desire to believe something, he portrays man as caught between an unavoidable skepticism and an unbelievable skepticism:

> What a chimera then is man! What a novelty! What a monster, what a chaos, what a contradiction, what a prodigy! Judge of all things, imbecile worm of the earth; depositary of truth, a sink of uncertainty and error; the pride and refuse of the universe.
>
> Who will unravel this tangle? Nature confutes the skeptics, and reason confutes the dogmatists. What then will you become, O men! who try to find out by your natural reason what is your true condition? You cannot avoid one of these sects, nor adhere to one of them.

Know then, proud man, what a paradox you are to yourself. Humble yourself, weak reason: be silent foolish nature; learn that man infinitely transcends man, and learn from your Master your true condition, of which you are ignorant. Hear God![15]

When one hears God or has the faith that one hears God, then, as Pascal indicates in *pensée* 835–565 the prophecies, the miracles, and the proofs of our religion "are not of such a nature that they can be said to be absolutely convincing." Faith has not overcome the possibility of skeptical doubt. "But they are also of such a kind that it cannot be said that it is unreasonable to believe them." So, there is both evidence and obscurity to enlighten some and confuse others. Reason does not make one accept the religious truths, but they are not unreasonable. If one accepts them, it is grace, not reason, that leads to this acceptance. If one refuses to accept them, it is lust or malice of heart that leads to the rejection. "There is sufficient evidence to condemn, and insufficient to convince."[16] So, one believes by faith, or one disbelieves by bad character.

A problem has existed for both Pascal and Kierkegaard: What if one hears the wrong message, or nothing, or one's own inner rumblings? What if one makes the leap into faith and lands in just a human fantasyland? For Pascal, it is presented that if one just listens, after going through the skeptical purging of one's rational pretensions, God can and may reveal THE MESSAGE. For Kierkegaard, if one destroys one's rational pretensions, if one nonetheless realizes the need for a belief, one then actively makes the leap. But, one may fall flat on one's face or fall where one started or leap into demonic insanity. All sorts of results are possible.[17]

Before pursuing this from fideism to quietism, I should just like to make a brief historical excursion to report a recent discovery that was new to me, namely, that one of the most rational of Pascal's contemporaries, the Cambridge Platonist Ralph Cudworth, based his disproof of atheism on materials from Sextus Empiricus. Cudworth, in the stupefying 899 pages of *The True Intellectual*

System of the Universe (1678) uses Sextus as a source of all sorts of news about ancient beliefs. In the key section where Cudworth offers his disproof of atheism and his proof of the existence of God, Sextus is transformed from just a source into someone known as "Sextus the philosopher." This Sextus uses the Pyrrhonian weapons to undermine any credibility in the arguments for, or the evidence for, the denial of the existence of God.[18] Using Sextus in this way does not make Cudworth a fideist. But it is curious that he felt he first had to upgrade Sextus from a source to a philosopher to cite him in this crucial section much more than he cited Plato or anyone else to show the unreasonableness of atheism, even the irrationality of it. Then, and I think only then, could he proceed to present his peculiar version of the ontological argument.[19]

To return to my historical narrative, I shall discuss some seventeenth-century developments beyond fideism, namely, spiritualism or mysticism, especially in the form that this emerged in in the Christian quietists. Quietism has received limited and fairly negative treatment, mostly, I believe, because it has no base in the established churches.[20] The histories of it, usually very negative, trace it to the sixteenth-century Spanish mysticism of Santa Teresa of Avila and San Juan de la Cruz, who stressed the need to negate one's feelings and desires and to let God take over one's spirit.[21] The Catholic church was suspicious of the mystics since it saw that mystical practices could lead to individualistic religious views and to denial of the need for church activities. The spiritual force of the early Jesuits and of the Carmelites of Santa Teresa was so powerful and so important in providing the vitality, the living religion of Catholicism, that powered the Counter-Reformation that the Church channeled this mysticism into institutional forms—the Society of Jesus and the Carmelites—rather than suppressing it.

The dangers inherent in this kind of mysticism became apparent in the efforts of two leading spiritual leaders in the mid-seventeenth century, Miguel de Molinos and Jean de Labadie. Molinos was born in Spain in 1627. In 1669 he went to Italy, where he became a great success as a preacher and spiritual adviser. He became a close friend of the future Pope Innocent XI and lodged in the Vatican. Queen Christina of Sweden, living in Rome as a convert to Catholicism, chose Molinos as her spiritual adviser. He had a tremendous following in Italy. His teachings were hailed by many as a new religion, though he carefully stated his views as being those of Santa Teresa and San Juan de la Cruz. His book *The Spiritual Guide* (1675) was soon translated into Italian, French, Latin, German, and English.[22]

Gilbert Burnet, who became the Bishop of Salisbury, was in Rome then, and he summed up Molinos's view as "That in our Prayers and other Devotions, the best methods are to retire the mind from all gross Images, and to form an Act of Faith [an auto de fe!], and thereby to present ourselves before God, and then to sink into a Silence or Cessation of new Acts, and to let God act upon us, and so follow His Conduct."[23] An *auto de fe* was the proceeding by which heretics were condemned and then burned at the stake by the Spanish Inquisition.

Jesuits quickly saw that Molinos was minimizing or eliminating the role of church activities, prayer, penitence, and maybe even Communion. Molinos himself refused to hear confession from his followers, believing that if they were real quietists, God, not they themselves, was directing their activities. Hence, they had nothing to confess. One of Molinos's opponents indicated that there would then be no need for the church. Any moral aberration, including fornication between a priest and a nun, could be excused if the persons had given over control of their activities to God.[24]

After ten years of complaints, especially by Jesuits, Molinos was called before the Roman Inquisition. Twenty thousand letters to him from followers, mainly female, were seized (including two hundred from Queen Christina). He remained in prison (where Christina sent him clean laundry and food).[25] In 1687 he was condemned for having taught and practiced "godless doctrines" and doctrines "dangerous and destructive of Christian morality."[26] It was rumored that the letters showed he gave spiritual advice during sexual encounters, and that he was a libertine, debauching the finest ladies of Rome. It was rumored that he was not even a Christian, but that he was a Jew who had never even been baptized.[27]

Although his condemnation was very public, and he recanted at the same place Galileo had, Molinos was sentenced to life in prison. Even to this day the documentary evidence has not been published or available for inspection. Sixty-eight of his theses were condemned, and his reputation was sullied for the next three centuries.[28]

His views, which he insisted were those of Santa Teresa and San Juan de la Cruz, indicate both the spiritual force of this kind of skepticism and the possibility that it will lead beyond and outside of Christianity. H. C. Lea, the famous historian of the Spanish Inquisition, claimed that Spanish mysticism, which first appeared around 1500, was originally just a cover or fig leaf to allow forcibly converted priests and nuns to carry on their sex lives. When they were arrested *in flagrante dilecto*, they offered as a defense that they were illuminated and carried away by God. Lea traced the history of the *alumbrados* (illuminated persons) from fakery to genuine piety in the course of the sixteenth century.[29] In the teachings of Luis de Leon, Santa Teresa, and San Juan de la Cruz, Spanish mysticism became a most forceful personal involvement in religious experience. Its early exponents were mainly from the forced converts in Spain, who may have found it easier to reach God through mysticism than through the Church.[30] The revival of this view by Molinos came at a time when mystical movements were battering the established worlds of Protestantism as well as French Catholicism. The emphasis on denying one's desires, motives, and reasons and on opening oneself totally to God (while living in the world) made the need for established churches, creeds, and organized activities questionable.

I do not know if Molinos was a fake, a fraud, a great mystic, or a secret subversive agent against the church. His movement and his book, the *Guide*, had a great effect throughout Europe and America.[31] Associated Protestant movements spelled out, in more philosophical terms, the ultimate skepticism involved in quietism, and the final formulation went beyond all creeds and teachings.

The central Protestant figure, Jean de Labadie, has been treated as a misfit, a troublemaker, and a nut. (There is a very rare volume, a German history of heretics and fanatics of 1702, that has a rogue's gallery of most of the people I am discussing. Labadie's picture is labeled "archfanatic.")[32] Only in 1987 has a full, documented study of his life, career, and influence appeared.[33]

He was born in 1610 in southwestern France. He studied at the same high school that Montaigne had attended. Then he became a Jesuit. After further study, he left the Jesuits in 1639 and became involved with the Carmelites of Santa Teresa. He took the name Saint John of Christ and proclaimed that the Reign of Grace, the Divine Kingdom, would begin before 1666. He joined the Jansenists at Port-Royal during their persecution. The Catholic authorities were suspicious of his views and their possible effects. Labadie left Catholicism and became a Calvinist. He preached and taught in Geneva, where he greatly influenced such religious figures as Jakob Spener, the founder of Lutheran pietism.[34] Labadie became a minister in the Netherlands and is supposed to have preached to a thousand people in 1666 that the King of the Jews (Sabbatai Zevi) had arrived.[35] The most learned woman of the time, Anna Maria van Schurman (who knew twenty languages and wrote an Ethiopic grammar), joined him and helped formulate the very antirational, skeptical attack on theology, philosophy, and science that was part of the path to genuine religion.[36] According to their teachings, people's souls should be made bare so that God can act immediately on them. Labadie and Anna Maria van Schurman fought with the more rationalistic Calvinists in the Netherlands, and finally in 1668 they broke with Calvinism and founded their own sect. They were driven out of tolerant Holland in 1670, so they must have been pretty obnoxious. They moved in with Princess Elisabeth of the Palatine, the niece of Charles I of England.[37] Princess Elisabeth had been a friend and critic of Descartes. She became the abbotress of a medieval abbey at Herford, near Munster, in Germany, where she had taken in various *Chrétiens sans église*,[38] like Quakers, Mennonites, and Socinians, and she was happy to have her old friend Anna Maria van Schurman and the notorious Labadie as guests also.[39] There is a wonderful picture of the hothouse atmosphere of unaffiliated religion at Herford given in William Penn's journal of his trip to Holland and Germany.[40] Labadie eventually left and set up a commune at Altona outside Hamburg, where he died in 1674.[41]

The Labadie–van Schurman view was first an aggressive skepticism against any rational foundations for belief. (As far back as 1640, van Schurman led the attack against Cartesianism at the University of Utrecht.[42] She is supposed to have gotten furious about Descartes when he came into her house and found her reading Genesis in Hebrew. He looked at the text and said he once tried to make sense of it but could not. And so he turned to physics instead!)[43] As another quietist, Pierre Poiret, put it, reason must be placed on the dunghill and destroyed, so that God's actions can take over one's soul.[44] Poiret developed a violent skepticism, a way of negation of all of one's beliefs, to open oneself totally to God. And in so doing, Poiret, unlike van Schurman, became, in the end, a Cartesian by faith, instead of by reason, because that was what God revealed to him.[45]

Some of these quietists, in turning against all reason or belief, also turned against Scripture as a necessary aid to salvation, and against any religious laws or ceremonies. They denied the need for any sabbath observances, and they insisted that from the human point of view all days are equal. They rejected all existing Christian churches as degenerate and irrelevant to the spiritual life, though they saw themselves as ardent, pious Christians.[46] Instead they set up a communist community, where everyone's life was dominated by the immediate action of the Holy Spirit upon them. Two Labadist colonies were set up in the New World, perhaps the first utopian communist communities in America.[47]

The quietism of Molinos and of Labadie, van Schurman, and

Poiret led beyond and maybe outside Christianity. By denying all human bases for finding religious truth, by denying all human rational activities, they turned themselves over solely to divine influence. They saw churches, observances, and Scripture as unnecessary human ways of trying to bridge the gulf between the human and the divine—unnecessary and even dangerous, since corrupt human beings could misdirect and misuse the situation. As a recent Spanish study of Molinos suggests, the logic of quietist mysticism eliminates any source of knowledge except direct revelation from God.[48] This can then make Jesus and Mary unnecessary as intermediaries. When one reaches this point, one is beyond Christianity and outside of it, just pursuing the unrestricted mystical path to opening oneself to God.

A further element in the theology of Labadie and Anna Maria van Schurman is their relationship to seventeenth-century Judaism. This has hardly been explored, and I will mention only one point.

A Jewish development that was quite important to them was the messianic movement of 1666. As a Catholic, Labadie had preached that the Millennium, the thousand-year reign of Christ, would begin by 1666. At the beginning of 1666, the Jews of Amsterdam received news from the Near East that the Messianic Age had begun, and that the long-awaited Jewish messiah had arrived in the person of Sabbatai Zevi of Smyrna. Sabbatai Zevi himself wrote to the Amsterdam Jewish community telling them of his initial pronouncements for the Messianic Age and of his appointment of the new kings of the earth. Over 90 percent of the Jewish world in Asia, Africa, and Europe accepted Sabbatai Zevi as the long-awaited messiah.[49] He was greeted with almost total acceptance in Amsterdam and Hamburg, two centers of the Spanish and Portuguese Jews. People made plans to set off for the Holy Land as soon as Sabbatai would call them. The Amsterdam stock exchange (the first in Europe) went crazy, since no one knew whether to buy or sell in the Messianic Age.[50]

Millenarian Christians were also greatly affected. Some accepted Sabbatai Zevi as the Messiah, some as the forerunner of

Jesus' return. One of the first accounts of the reaction in Holland to the news about Sabbatai Zevi appears in a letter by Peter Serrarius, an Amsterdam merchant and divine who was Spinoza's patron, to John Dury, a Scottish Millenarian who had been trying all his life to reunite all of the Christian churches in preparation for the Millenium. Serrarius told Dury that the King of the Jews had arrived and that Labadie had preached to a thousand people about it.[51] Labadie was apparently very excited by the event. He wrote a now very rare work about what this meant, concluding that God was rewarding the Jews for their patience and suffering, while showing up the failure of Christians to be ready for their final event.[52] It is my suspicion that part of the reason for Labadie's break with the Calvinists and his exile from Holland was that he was an aggressive Sabbatian, seeing Sabbatai's career as an important sign of God's relations to man.[53]

Sabbatai Zevi was arrested by the sultan and threatened with death. He converted to Islam and became a minor Ottoman official. He was still accepted by some Jewish and Christian followers who, as Serrarius puts it, recognized that this showed that God works in marvelous ways.[54] Most Jews rejected Sabbatai after his conversion, though some insisted that it was part of his messianic mission that he had to take on the sins of mankind by becoming an apostate, and that he would return as a pious Jew. He died in 1676 while attending a Yom Kippur service in Montenegro.[55] Today, his followers are awaiting his second coming and the full flowering of the Messianic Age.[56]

The case of Sabbatai Zevi generated a skeptical attack against Judaism. John Evelyn published a work in 1669, *The Three Imposters*, which presents Sabbatai as the greatest fraud of them all.[57] And the case was seen by Christians seeking to convert Jews as evidence that Jews could not tell a real messiah from a false one, and hence they should accept the Christian messiah.[58] For the purposes of this essay, one of the most interesting and least studied discussions of the skeptical impact of the Sabbatai Zevi case appeared in a rather amazing work, *Letters Writ by a Turkish Spy at Paris*, covering the period 1637–82. The author of the first part was G. P. Marana of Genoa. The remainder, more than six volumes, first appeared in English in the 1690s; its author or authors are still not known.[59] A ninth volume, apparently by Daniel Defoe, carries the story up to 1693.[60] The work is the first of the genre of an outsider criticizing and poking fun at European ideas, values, and beliefs. It was the inspiration for Montesquieu's *Persian Letters* and other such Enlightenment criticisms of the European world.[61] The *Turkish Spy* was extremely popular. It appeared in French, Dutch, German, and Russian, as well as the original Italian and English, and it was republished until 1801, the thirty-first edition.[62]

Although the work must have been a best-seller, it is hardly studied for its content and influence. One of its subjects is the interchange over thirty years between the Spy and the sultan's agent in Vienna, a Jew, Nathan ben Saddi. Nathan in the story becomes an ardent follower of Sabbatai Zevi. The Spy keeps proclaiming through the work that he is not trying to convert Nathan to Islam but, instead, to reason. "Do not suspect me of Partiality," the Spy says, "or that I am fond of making Proselytes, because I take such Pains to restore thee to *reason*, and make thee sensible thou art a Man."[63] The Spy insists both he and Nathan need to get free of their errors and improve themselves. Nathan had gone berserk during the Sabbatai Zevi episode. The Spy rails at him: "How many Messiahs have ye had. Twenty-Five at least, besides the Son of Mary. . . . Must all the World be bothered to Eternity by the Fables of your Nation?"[64]

The Spy argues in his letters to Nathan that Judaism is based on a false history of the world: It is just one more man-made religion, based on corrupted or truncated documents. The so-called oral Law of the Talmud is just a collection of rabbinical opinions with no divine sanction. All the documents, the Koran, the Bible, and the Talmud, "were penn'd by Men as liable to Temptations and Errors of all Sorts, as Thou and I."[65] So, one should use one's reason rather than depend on such writings.

After a fairly lengthy attack on the importance of the Talmud, the Spy presents a version of the pre-Adamite theory to show why one should not accept Genesis as true history. The Spy's brother had traveled to China and India and had found people there had much different histories of the world and different scriptures. The Chinese and Indians believe the world to be much older than the Jews do, and they believe there were people long before the biblical Adam. (It is curious that the evidence adduced by the Spy, attributed to his brother, contains a lot of details about Oriental religion and cosmology that were not in the European literature until the late eighteenth century.)[66] All of this is supposed to show that Judaism is just one religion among many, having no privileged status. Instead of being taken in by its claims to uniqueness and superiority, someone like Nathan should use his reason. The Spy had learned about the rational religion from the Wandering Jew, Ahasuerus, who, we are told, came to Paris in 1644 and talked at length with the Spy.[67] (This is one of the first appearances of the Wandering Jew in European fiction.)[68] Later on, the Wandering Jew finds the Lost Tribes of Israel in the northern parts of Asia, and they are practicing the original and best religion. "They are a nation of philosophers."[69] They have a kind of socialist communal life. They are pacifists and vegetarians. They flourish because of their "exquisite temperance and moderation in all things." They have the rational religion, a pure philosophical Judaism, which would be accepted if we used our reason. We would realize "there is but *One Law*, and *One Thing* necessary to men, that is To Live according to *Reason*. This is engraven in every Man's Heart, and there needs no *Comment* to explain it. Thou art a sufficient *Law-giver, Rabbi, Doctor* and *Interpreter* to Thyself."[70]

In another essay, I suggest that what the Spy was doing was inventing Reformed Judaism out of ideas of Isaac La Peyrère and Spinoza. This rational Reformed Judaism emerged from the Spy's critique of Orthodox or normative Judaism.[71] It is again a religion beyond the traditional limits of Judaism and is an early formulation of the religion of reason, developed from a skepticism about

Judaism. The skeptical road to this religion of reason came out of, I believe, the Bible criticism developed by Hobbes, by the Quaker Samuel Fisher, by Spinoza, and by Father Richard Simon.[72]

Hobbes, in *Leviathan* (1651), put in print the historical question, Is it possible that Moses did not write all of the text of the Five Books of Moses? In the formulation offered, Hobbes says he accepts the Church of England's claim that the Books are God's message to mankind. He only asks, Could Moses have written all that is attributed to him, considering that this includes the verses describing the death of Moses and some events that happened thereafter?[73] Whatever Hobbes himself might have believed, or not believed, he expresses no doubts about the message but just suggests historically that someone else must have written part of the text.[74]

The problem of the questioning of the Mosaic authorship became the beginning of a kind of religious skepticism as it was presented by La Peyrère and then developed by Fisher and Spinoza. Hobbes may well have gotten his question from La Peyrère, who was in Paris when Hobbes was, and who was a friend of Father Mersenne, Gassendi, and others whom Hobbes knew. La Peyrère, the secretary of the Prince of Conde, wrote a large work around 1641 offering a weird Jewish-Christian messianic theory. As the way of justifying his theory, he questions the accuracy of the present text of Scripture and whether Scripture is the history of mankind or just the history of the Jews.[75]

The questioning of the accuracy of the text was developed by La Peyrère first from pointing out conflicts in the text, starting with the problem of who was Cain's wife, and then following with various conflicting passages from the two creation stories. He pointed out that various books are mentioned in Scripture that are not in the present text. From all of this, La Peyrère built up some of the basic elements of higher biblical criticism. The text we now have has been changed by various copyists. Present copied texts have thousands of variant readings. Several source versions have been put together so that some confusion resulted.

We do not have an accurate text but only a "heap of Copie confusedly taken."[76]

And, on another side, we have ample evidence that the Bible cannot be the history of all of mankind. Various cultures, the Chinese, Mexican, Polynesian, and others, have different chronologies and different histories. They have monuments that predate any event in the Bible. Both from the Bible and from information about non-Jewish ancient cultures and present non-European cultures, it is evident, according to La Peyrère, that all of the people in the world cannot be descendants of Adam and Eve. Hence, there must have been people before Adam, and the varieties of human existence must be due to polygenetic developments.[77]

According to La Peyrère, the Bible is only the history of the Jews, not the history of all mankind. As such, it shows how God created the Jews, with Adam as their progenitor (after an endless period of people living in a state of nature). God elected the Jews then rejected them at the time of Jesus. He grafted the Gentiles to their stock and now is about to recall them to the center stage of world history to rule the world from Jerusalem with the Jewish Messiah and his regent, the king of France.[78]

La Peyrère's Bible criticism (not his messianism) was taken over by Spinoza and Samuel Fisher. Historically, Spinoza seems to have learned about La Peyrère's theory before his excommunication and used elements of it in the *Tractatus Theologico-Politicus*.[79] Fisher apparently knew Spinoza and worked with him on translating some Quaker tracts into Hebrew shortly after the excommunication.[80] Spinoza intensified the textual problems that had to be explained since, unlike La Peyrère, he knew Hebrew. He and Fisher made a central issue the epistemological problem of finding the Word of God in a historical document. They not only underscored the historical problem of how an ancient text was transmitted to present-day readers and how all sorts of faults and errors could have crept in; they also pointed out that finding the Word of God in Scripture involves being able to tell that a set of words correspond to God's message. This can only be done if one antecedently knows God's message. So, a physical object—a Torah scroll, or a Bible manuscript, or a printed Bible—could only be determined to be God's Word if one independently knows his or her Word.[81]

That the Word is something different from a set of statements in the Bible, Fisher and Spinoza contended, is evident from the fact that prior to the availability of the written Word people knew God's message—people such as Abel, Noah, and Abraham.[82] Also, they both contended that people outside the whole Judeo-Christian framework, like the Native Americans and the sages of ancient Greece, could know the Word without knowing the Bible.[83]

Spinoza also questioned the possibility that the authors of Scripture had some special knowledge or insight that other people do not have. His questioning of the possibility of "prophetic knowledge" and of "prophets" is part of this critique.[84]

The end result, in the presentations of Fisher (in a nine-hundred-page attack on the Calvinist theory of religious knowledge)[85] and of Spinoza, is a skepticism about the possibility of obtaining religious knowledge from a document that exists in time and space and that was written by human beings, copied by others, and read by us. The English Puritans tried to avoid the problem by declaring, in the Westminster Confession of 1658, that God preserved the text exactly in all of its transmissions but also preserved the Message in all of the translations.[86] This role of God as guarantor and conservator is somewhat like the Cartesian deity conserving and preserving mathematical truths, except that there is a problem because of the variants in the preserved texts. Mathematical truths are presumably universal and eternal. Bible texts are man-made objects, historically created under historical circumstances. And these texts vary from one another. Which is the right text? Spinoza would claim one could only tell by which conforms to the rational understanding of God's message, an understanding independent of any particular historical text.[87]

Fisher would claim it depended on reading the text in terms of the spirit within.[88]

If it is claimed that some texts contain divine inspiration, then which are they? Father Richard Simon, who followed up the Hobbes–La Peyrère–Spinoza line of examination of Scripture, said that he agreed with Spinoza's method, but not his conclusion, because the Bible is an inspired document. Then Simon, who knew far more than the others about the historical problems involved, sadly said that he did not know if any of the extant texts were inspired. The problem of getting to, or back to, the inspired text involved overcoming probably unsolvable epistemological problems about knowing past facts with certainty.[89]

The religious skepticism generated about knowing God through, or by means of, historical documents resulted, on the one hand, in the antibiblicism of the deists, who reduced the historical religious documents to the status of any other historical writings;[90] or, on the other hand, in Kierkegaard's fideism concerning how a historical point of departure is possible for an eternal consciousness. Logically or historically, it is not possible, but by faith such a point of departure is the core of one's religion.[91]

To return to an earlier theme, if doubts about messianic Judaism, because of the fiasco over Sabbatai Zevi, led to proposing a religion of reason, doubts about Christian messianism led to a formulation of a Jewish version of Christianity that became a religion of ethics. Jewish doubts about Christian messianic claims go back to the beginnings of Christianity. Christian authorities tried for centuries to get rid of the doubts and the doubters, only too often by force and violence. As a result, Jewish doubts were not published. In the late Renaissance it apparently became somewhat safe to write these down and circulate them. A medieval account of the Jewish life of Jesus began to be known in the European world in Elizabethan times. Christopher Marlowe had access either to this text or to themes in it and is supposed to have taken material from it for his purported atheistic lecture given at Sir Walter Raleigh's home.[92] The work was published in the late seventeenth century in two versions by German anti-Semitic theologians to show how nasty the Jews were.[93]

A more impressive case of Jewish doubts about Christianity appears in the *Colloquium Heptaplomeres* of the great French jurist Jean Bodin. This is a dialogue written around 1580–90 between a Catholic, a Lutheran, a Calvinist, a Jew, a Moslem, and two pagans about which is the true religion. The shocker in this is that the Jew wins![94] Bodin did not publish the work. When he died, he was denounced as a Jew or as a Judaizer. When the dialogues surfaced, people were sure he must have been Jewish to raise so many questions against Christianity. Bodin's dialogues were not published until 1841, but they became known all over Europe in the period 1650–1700. Bodin's heirs got into a legal fight about who owned the manuscript. When the case came before a judge in Paris, the judge took the manuscript home and had it copied. His friends copied it from his copy. A copy got to England when Henry Oldenburg copied a Paris copy. John Milton apparently got a copy of Oldenburg's copy. Later Milton's copy got to Germany, where it was sent to John Dury. And so, G. W. Leibniz and his associates were preparing a copy for publication (which never was published). The work was considered too audacious to be printed,[95] but, judging from the number of known copies, it was studied all over the learned world.[96] And it made known the objections to Christian messianic claims that can be based on traditional Jewish materials.

A stronger collection of Jewish arguments against Christianity were set forth by members of the Spanish-Portuguese Jewish community in Amsterdam. Most of the early members of this group were born and reared in Spain or Portugal as Catholics. Many of them were persecuted by the Inquisition for secretly carrying on Jewish practices. Some of those who escaped and ended up in Holland found they were safe and could argue against their tormentors. An amazing literature, mostly in Spanish and Portuguese, was written during the seventeenth century, polemically attacking basic Christian claims.[97] Perhaps the climax of this was the public debate between Isaac Orobio de Castro and Philip van Limborch over the truth of the Christian religion (a debate that John Locke apparently attended).[98] Orobio typifies the kind of Jewish arguer who emerged in Amsterdam. He had been a royal physician in Spain and a professor of scholastic metaphysics. He was imprisoned and tortured for three years because a servant reported he "Judaized," that is, carried on some form of Jewish behavior. After being released, he escaped to France where he became a professor at the medical school of the University of Toulouse. He had to live there as a Christian. Finally he disappeared and surfaced in Amsterdam, where he joined the Jewish community and circumcised himself. He wrote strong philosophical attacks on Jewish backsliders and Christian apologists, and he wrote the only important Jewish answer of the time to Spinoza.[99] His most important work is a lengthy polemic arguing that, no matter how it looks, God is on the side of the Jews, that he has preserved them and will redeem them, and that the Christians are mistaken.[100]

The chief rabbi of Amsterdam, Saul Levi Mortera, notorious for his role in excommunicating Spinoza, grew up in Venice and as a court secretary at the Louvre in Paris. He argued against Christians, and in 1660, he wrote a huge Portuguese work challenging the evidence offered by Christians to establish that Jesus is the expected Jewish Messiah.[101]

None of the Amsterdam polemics were published at the time, but they circulated in elegant manuscript copies. (Orobio said he sent a copy of his masterpiece to the Jesuits in Brussels, who liked it very much.)[102] Only in the late Enlightenment were some published, but most of these polemics still remain in manuscripts in libraries all over the world. The principal items are now being prepared for publication.[103]

The Amsterdam polemics were not rabbinical nit-picking. They were hard-nosed attacks, using the philosophical and theological weapons of the Christian community to raise doubts about the truth of Christianity, both from within the Biblical context and from the evidences of world history. When these documents passed into general circulation, they had the effect of justifying the return to Judaism of the persecuted Iberians and of seriously challenging Christians. The first documents appeared in an auction in 1715 in the Hague.[104] As an example, a New England preacher, George Bethune English, found some of these manuscripts in the Harvard theological collection in the late eighteenth century. He studied them, went to New York to consult a rabbi about them, and then wrote an attack on Christianity. He was forced to resign his post and then was seen getting off a boat in Egypt and putting on a fez. He later became a Turkish spy.[105]

The Jewish anti-Christian polemics were used by French atheists like Baron d'Holbach to attack Christianity. (He published an abbreviated version of Orobio's text entitled *Israel vengé*.)[106] These polemics were considered the strongest intellectual evidence against Christianity.[107] They led to the development of a Jewish version of Christianity that would see both Judaism and Christianity as primarily ethical views, no longer providing any supernatural religious knowledge.

The skeptical critique of the possibility of knowledge beyond immediate experience in the sixteenth century led to the formulation of fideism. Regardless of the skeptical problems involved in obtaining knowledge, religious knowledge could be obtained by faith. The quietists carried this further, by insisting on the need to actively empty one's mind so that God can, if he or she so desires, provide any content about natural or religious matters. Opponents of both the fideists and the quietists saw clear and imminent danger that no assurance can be given for any particular religious belief and that no institutional religious activities are necessary. The quietism of Labadie and van Schurmann ended up beyond any specific creeds or practices.

At the same time, the Bible criticism of Hobbes, La Peyrère, Fisher, Spinoza, and Father Simon created another kind of skepticism, a doubt about whether the main religious document of the West could provide any assured knowledge about the nature and destiny of man. The debacle of Jewish messianism, and the Jewish critique of Christianity, seemed to undermine the bases for the views of Jews and Christians, based on any historical events of the past and future. Another side of the story, which I shall not go into here, is the skepticism raised by becoming aware of the plurality of religious belief all over the planet. An optimistic way of dealing with this, claiming that these are all variations on the true religion, Judeo-Christianity, was rapidly followed by the view of the English deists that all religions are forms of natural religion, which is basically a moral code.[108]

The kinds of skepticism introduced into the quest of religious knowledge in the seventeenth and eighteenth centuries undermined the traditional rational evidence for the existence of God and for the knowledge of his or her nature. The skeptical probing of the roots of historical religion, especially as proposed by Jews and Christians, questioned whether there was any way of bridging the fallible information about human events to reach knowledge of God. All that seemed to be left were the moral teachings, which, as Spinoza had already said, could be known independently of any religious tradition.[109]

Historically, one of the major consequences was the development of antireligion, atheism, in the Enlightenment, which reached its climax in the claims that there is no need for the God hypothesis, that Jesus never existed, that Moses was a conman, and that religions are just man-made belief systems perpetrated by the priesthood.[110] The underground work *The Three Imposters, Moses, Jesus, and Mohammed; or The Spirit of M. Spinoza* became the complete rejection of the religious heritage of the West.[111]

In closing I should like to suggest that other alternatives existed and do exist for dealing with the results of religious skepticism. Kierkegaard wrote in full awareness of the most radical claims of the Bible critics and the interpreters of religion as man-made. He did not ignore them but presented fideism in a form in which it could function, without denying the modern intellectual world.[112] Fundamentalism began as another way of rejecting the irreligious conclusions and presented an age of revelation to answer the age of reason.[113] (It is hardly recognized outside of fundamentalist circles that at the same time that the Enlightenment freethinkers were criticizing religious belief there was a tremendous outpouring of millennial interpretation of the Bible, contending that the culmination of human history was at hand and that this literature was written by highly intellectual scholars of the time.)[114]

My own conviction is that the most positive and promising note to be sounded was in the creedless spiritualism that was offered by Labadie and Anna Maria van Schurman, combined with a Jewish reading of Christianity: to wit, as rabbi Nathan Shapira of Jerusalem told the Christian Millenarians of Amsterdam, the Sermon on the Mount is the finest teachings of our rabbis;[115] and as Moses Germanus, an ex-Jesuit, ex-pietist, ex-Christian Kabbalist turned rabbi, claimed, Jesus was a great rabbi teaching the finest morality whose life got turned into a theodicy by human misunderstanding.[116] Jewish Christianity could perhaps provide a content for creedless spiritualism without needing a questionable metaphysical theology or questionable history to sustain it. This moral rendition of Christianity, like the Turkish Spy's rational rendition of Judaism, presents another form of religion beyond Judaism and Christianity, a form that I call religious humanism.

It is a commonplace view of irreligious or antireligious Enlightenment folk that mankind has gone from superstition and magic, to religion, to a scientific understanding of the world. What I should like to suggest as the summation of my story is that within seventeenth-century Judaism and Christianity, certain developments took place that went beyond traditional formulations, ceremonies, established religious creeds, and institutions, and that these presented a universalistic, creedless mysticism and sense of community and the moral essence of Judaism and Christianity. These forms of religious humanism did not fall victim to the Enlightenment trashing of organized and institutional religion. Rather, they provided much of the push for the abolition of slavery, for the utopian experiences in America, and for an enlightened moral order both then and now (in the many human-rights and relief agencies).

Much, maybe too much, attention is given to the warfare between organized, institutional religion and the new science and philosophy of the seventeenth century. Galileo and Molinos both recanted in the same place. Galileo became the martyr for the scientific enlightenment, Molinos for the unaffiliated spiritual people (mainly former Protestants). What the universalism of Samuel Fisher and Spinoza, the unattached communal spiritualism of the quietists, and the rational and moral readings of Judaism and Christianity represented has generally been ignored. Those who took these paths preserved some of the vital and essential features of Judaism and Christianity without the institutional framework. They did not get into great confrontations with the Enlightenment atheists or the antireligious Darwinians. Perhaps in studying those who took these paths in the seventeenth century, we may find both a better understanding of what happened then and some useful guidance for what we can and should do now. We might find a skeptical faith, the outcome of several skeptical crises, for our skeptical age. But, of course, a skeptical believer like myself has always the haunting possibility that creedless, unaffiliated belief can become either idiosyncratic or insane. So, the skeptic has to have faith that his faith will not become fanaticism and must be constantly on guard. This may not be the most secure situation, but I think it emerges from the massive waves of doubts, epistemological and historical, that washed over traditional belief in the seventeenth and eighteenth centuries. It may last longer and provide more basis for commitment than the "firm" commitments that have lost their vitality or that have become counterproductive to the human situation.

Notes

1. Cf. Richard H. Popkin, *The History of Scepticism from Erasmus to Spinoza* (Berkeley and Los Angeles: University of California Press, 1979), chaps. 1–2; and idem, "Scepticism in Modern Thought," *Dictionary of the History of Ideas* (New York: Charles Scribner's Sons, 1973), pp. 240–51.

2. Popkin, *History of Scepticism*, chap. 1.

3. Ibid., chap. 3.

4. Ibid., pp. 46–47.

5. Ibid., pp. 34–35.

6. Ibid., pp. 36–41. Francisco Sanches's text has just appeared in English: *That Nothing Is Known*, translated by Douglas F. S. Thomson, with an introduction and notes by Elaine Limbrick (New York: Cambridge University Press, 1988).

7. Ibid., pp. 54–55.

8. Pierre Charron, *Les Trois Véritez* (Paris: Du Corroy, 1595); and Popkin, *History of Scepticism*, pp. 56–59.

9. Pierre Charron, *De la Sagesse* (Paris, 1606), bks. 1–2.

10. Popkin, *History of Scepticism*, chap. 4; and idem, "Scepticism and the Counter-Reformation in France," *Archiv fur Reformations Geschichte* 51 (1960): 58–88.

11. Cf. Popkin, *History of Scepticism*, pp. 90–93; and idem, "La Mothe le Vayer, François," in *Encyclopedia of Philosophy*, 4: 67–68.

12. Cf. Blaise Pascal, "Entretiens avec M. de Saci," in *Oeuvres* Lafuma edition (Paris and New York: Macmillan, 1963), pp. 291–97; and R. H. Popkin, ed., *Pascal Selections* (New York: Macmillan, 1989), pp. 79–89.

13. Cf. R. H. Popkin, "Pascal, Blaise," in *Encyclopedia of Philosophy*, 6:51–55; and Introduction to *Pascal Selections*, pp. 1–17.

14. Blaise Pascal, *Pensées*, 131–434, in *Selections*, p. 211.

15. Ibid., p. 212.

16. Pascal, *Pensées*, 835–564, in *Selections*, p. 263.

17. Cf. R. H. Popkin, "Theological and Religious Scepticism," *Christian Scholar* 39 (1956): 150–58; and idem, "Kierkegaard and Scepticism," in *Kierkegaard: A Collection of Critical Essays*, ed. Josiah Thompson (New York: Doubleday, 1972), pp. 342–73.

18. Ralph Cudworth, *The True Intellectual System of the Universe* (London: Richard Royston, 1678), pp. 692–96.

19. Ibid., p. 696ff.

20. Cf. Leszek Kolakowski, "Quietism," in *Encyclopedia of Religion*, 12:153–55.

21. See, for instance, "Quietism," in *New Catholique Encyclopedia*, 12:26–28; and "Quietisme," in *Dictionnaire de Théologie Catholique*, 13:1554–73.

22. On the biography of Molinos, see E. Pacho's article "Molinos," in *Dictionnaire de Spiritualité ascetique et mystique* (Paris: Beauchesne, 1977–80), vol. 10, pt. 2, pp. 1486–1514; José Angel Valente, "Ensayo sobre Miguel de Molinos," in *Miguel Molinos, Guia Espiritual* (Barcelona: Barral,

1974), pp. 28–40; and Paul Dudon, S.J., *Le Quietiste espagnol Michel Molinos (1628–1696)* (Paris: Beauchesne, 1921).

23. Gilbert Burnet, "Relating to the Affair of Molinos and Quietism," Letter I in *Three Letters Concerning the Present State of Italy Written in the Year 1687* (n.p., 1688), pp. 1–93. Molinos's doctrines are described on p. 29ff.

24. Cf. the accounts of Molinos's views in *Dictionnaire de Théologie Catholique*, 13: 1554–73; *Dictionnaire de Spiritualité*, vol. 12, pt. 2, pp. 1486–1515; and *Enciclopedia Universal illustrada*, 35:1528–31.

25. On Molinos's relations with Christina, see Sven Stolpe, *Christina of Sweden* (New York: Macmillan, 1966), pp. 307–31.

26. Text of the condemnation is given in the *Dictionnaire de Théologie Catholique*, 13: 1563–71. Burnet, *Three Letters*, gives the text of the censure of Molinos by the Inquisition (p. 67ff).

27. In Antonio Dominguez Ortiz, *Los Judeoconversos en Espana y America* (Madrid: Ediciones ISTMO, 1971), Molinos is described as "la ultima personalidad importante conversa desde el punto de vista religioso" (a *converso* is a Jewish convert). The note at this point reports that in the posted text of Molinos's condemnation in the churches of Madrid, he was described as "an Aragonese, descended from Jews." Burnet, *Three Letters*, reports that "because *Molinos* was by his birth a Spaniard, it has been given out of late, that perhaps he was descended of a *Jewish* or *Mahometan* Race, and that he might carry in his Blood, or in his first Education, some seeds of these Religions" (p. 28). See also Michel de Certeau, *Heterologies: Discourse on the Other* (Minneapolis: University of Minnesota Press, 1986), pp. 84–85.

It is curious that the only fact of Molinos's trip from Spain to Italy that is known is that when the boat stopped at Livorno, he got off and went to the Jewish ghetto there and then went to Rome. Cf. Justo Fernandez Alonso, "Una bibliografia inedita de Miguel Molinos," in *Anthologia Annua* (Rome: Institute Espanol de Historia Ecclesiastica, 1964), 12:293–321. This gives the text of a biography written by one of Molinos's supporters from the time of his condemnation. The item about his visit to the Jewish quarter in Livorno is on p. 301.

28. Cf. the account of Molinos's condemnation in *Dictionnaire de Théologie Catholique*, 13: 1563–71 (where the condemned doctrines are given in Latin and French); and *Dictionnaire de Spiritualité*, vol. 10, pt. 2, pp. 1507–10.

29. Henry Charles Lea, "Mystics and Illuminati," chap. 2 in *Chapters from the Religious History of Spain, Connected with the Inquisition* (Philadelphia: Lea Brothers, 1890).

30. On this, see Americo Castro, *La Realidad Historico de Espana* (Mexico: Editorial Porrua, 1966), p. 186ff.

31. See the list of editions and translations in the catalogues of the Bibliothèque Nationale and the British Library, and in the National Union Catalogue.

32. Jo. Frid. Corvinus, *Historia von denen Wider Tauffen: Anabaptiscum et Enthusiaticum, Pantheon* (n.p., 1702). The first picture is that of Labadie, "Archfanaticus."

33. T. J. Saxby, *The Quest for the New Jerusalem: Jean de Labadie and the Labadists, 1610–1744* (Dordrecht: Nijohff, 1987).

34. On the biographical details, see Saxby, *Quest for the New Jerusalem,* chaps. 1–10.

35. Ibid., p. 144. On this see Ernestine van der Wall's essay on the reaction of Peter Serrarius and Labadie to Sabbatai Zevi in *Pietismus und Neuzeit,* 14: 109–24, Wolfenbuttel Colloquium on Chilasmus in Germany and England in the Seventeenth Century, ed. Martin Brecht et al.; and John Dury's letter to Johann Ulrich in 1666, quoting a letter he had received from Serrarius, dated 23 July 1666, describing Labadie's sermon, Zurich, Staatsarchiv Ms. E. II 457e, fol. 995.

36. See Una Birch (Pope-Hennesey), *Anna van Schurman, Artist, Scholar, Saint* (New York: Longmans, 1909). See also van Schurman's autobiography, *Eucleria,* first published in Amsterdam in 1684 and republished in Leeuwarden in 1978, the three hundredth anniversary of her death.

37. See Saxby, *Quest for the New Jerusalem,* chap. 9.

38. On the unaffiliated Christians, see Leszek Kolakowski, *Chrétiens sans Eglise* (Paris: Gallimard, 1969).

39. See ibid., p. 758ff; and Saxby, *Quest for the New Jerusalem,* chap. 9.

40. William Penn, *An Account of W. Penn's Travails in Holland and Germany, Anno MDCLXXVII,* 2nd impression (London: T. Sowle, 1694), pp. 44–51.

41. Saxby, *Quest for the New Jerusalem,* chap. 10.

42. See Birch, *Anna van Schurman,* pp. 47, 53, 62; and van Schurman, *Eucleria,* p. 36ff. She is given credit for writing the speech of the rector, Gisbert Voetius, denouncing Descartes and Cartesianism. She is supposed to have attended the meeting of the Academic Senate of the

University of Utrecht, sitting behind a screen, since women were not allowed at such august gatherings.

43. See Birch, *Anna van Schurman*, p. 62ff.

44. Pierre Poiret, "Of Reason and Its Ideas," vol. 1, chap. 10, and "Of Faith, as It Respects the Understanding," vol. 5, chap. 4, in *The Divine Oeconomy; or, An Universal System of the Works and Purposes of God Towards Man, Demonstrated*, 6 vols. (London: R. Bonwicke, 1713), pp. 333–61, 93–108.

45. Poiret strongly denounced any form of rationalism, including Cartesianism, insisting that one had to empty one's mind, think of nothing, and turn to God. Then, through God's illumination, one could accept a kind of Cartesianism by revelation rather than reason. Cf. Kolakowski, *Chrétiens*, pp. 684–88; Pierre Poiret, *Cogitatum rationalium de Deo, Anima, et Malo* (Amsterdam, 1685); and idem, *De Eruditione triplici, solida, superficiaria et falsa* (Amsterdam, 1707).

Anna Maria van Schurman had said, "Il est donc de toute justice que nous retournions à Dieu par la voie contraire, c'est-à-dire en brisant le joug superbe de notre raison, et de notre orgueil, et de notre amour pervers, et en faisant profession de la plus complète abnégation et du plus entire abandon," published in A. Foucher de Careil, *Descartes et la Princess Palatine* (Paris: Auguste Durand, 1862), pp. 97–98.

46. Saxby, *Quest for the New Jerusalem*, chaps. 10–11. David Mason, *The Life of John Milton*, 7 vols. (London: Macmillan, 1877), 5:595, gives a list of beliefs of the Labadists as (1) God may and does deceive man; (2) Scripture is not necessary to salvation, the immediate action of the Spirit on souls being sufficient; (3) there ought to be no baptism of infants; (4) truly spiritual believers are not bound by law or ceremonies; (5) sabbath observance is unnecessary, all days being alike; and (6) the ordinary Christian church is degenerate and decrepit. A similar list appears in Jacques Basnage de Beauval, *Annales des Provinces-Unis* (The Hague, 1726), 2:53.

47. Saxby, *Quest for the New Jerusalem*, chaps. 12–13.

48. Cf. Valente, "Ensayo sobre Miguel de Molinos."

49. On Sabbatai Zevi's messianic career, see Gershom Scholem, *Sabbatai Sevi: The Mystical Messiah* (Princeton: Princeton University Press, 1973).

50. On this, see Scholem, *Sabbatai Sevi*, chap. 5; and Jonathan I. Israel, *European Jewry in the Age of Mercantilism, 1550–1750* (Oxford: Clarendon Press, 1985), chap. 9, sec. 1, pp. 206–16. Susanna Akerman has discussed

Queen Christina's involvement in the excitement over Sabbatai Zevi in *Queen Christina of Sweden and Her Circle* (Leiden: Brill, 1991).

51. Peter Serrarius to John Dury, Zurich, Staatsarchiv, Ms. E. II. 457e, fols. 747, 995. On Serrarius, see Ernestine van der Wall, *De Mystieke Chiliast Peter Serrarius (1600–1669) en zijn Wereld* (Leiden, 1987). An English translation of this important work is being prepared.

52. Jean de Labadie, *Jugement charitable et juste sur l'état présent des juifs* (Amsterdam 1667). Cf. Ernestine van der Wall, "A Precursor of Christ or a Jewish Imposter?" *Pietismus und Neuzeit* 14 (1988): 109–24.

53. There is, as yet, no known evidence of this. Saxby hardly discusses the effect of Sabbatai Zevi on Labadie's career.

54. See letter of Henry Oldenburg to Robert Boyle in Oldenburg's *Correspondence* (Madison and Milwaukee: University of Wisconsin Press, 1965), vol. 2, letter 652, pp. 446–47, where Serrarius is quoted to this effect.

55. On Sabbatai Zevi's conversion and its effects, see Scholem, *Sabbatai Sevi*, chaps. 6–8.

56. See Gershom Scholem's article "Doenmeh," *Encyclopedia Judaica*, 6: 148–51.

57. John Evelyn, *The History of the Three Late Famous Imposters* (London, 1669). The text is by Paul Rycaut, who was the English consul at Smyrna at the time.

58. See Charles Leslie, *A Short and Easy Method with the Jews*, vol. 1 of *Theological Works* (London, 1721), p. 52.

59. On Marana and the authorship of the later volumes, see Giovanni P. Marana, *Letters Writ by a Turkish Spy*, selected and edited by Arthur J. Weitzman (London: Routledge, 1970); and C. J. Betts, *Early Deism in France* (The Hague: Nijhoff, 1984), chap. 7.

60. [Daniel Defoe], *A Continuation of Letters Writ by a Turkish Spy at Paris, 1687–1693* (London, 1718).

61. Betts, *Early Deism*, chap. 7.

62. Cf. the lists of editions in the catalogues of the British Library and the Bibliothèque Nationale, and in the National Union Catalogue. The Russian edition, presumably done at the behest of Catherine the Great, is on microfilm at UCLA.

63. Marana, *Turkish Spy*, vol. 4, letter 5, pp. 251–52. (The pagination is the same in most editions.)

64. Ibid., vol. 6, letter 11, p. 235.

65. Ibid., vol. 5, letter 20, p. 203.

66. Cf. R. H. Popkin, *Isaac La Peyrère: His Life, His Work, and His Influence* (Leiden: Brill, 1987), pp. 115–21. These details about Oriental views also appear in the early parts of Charles Blount's *Oracle of Reason* of 1695 written by Blount or Charles Gliddon. This may indicate that the *Turkish Spy* was written by someone connected with the early English deists.

67. Marana, *Turkish Spy*, vol. 2, letter 1, pp. 177–78.

68. Cf. George K. Anderson, *The Legend of the Wandering Jew* (Providence: Brown University Press, 1970), p. 128.

69. Marana, *Turkish Spy*, vol. 6, letter 4, p. 215.

70. Ibid., vol. 5, letter 7, pp. 81–82.

71. Popkin, "A Late Seventeenth-Century Gentile Attempt to Convert the Jews to Reformed Judaism," in *Israel and the Nations: Essays Presented in Honor of Shmuel Ettinger*, ed. Shmuel Almog et al. (Jerusalem: Historical Society of Israel, 1987), pp. xxv–xlv.

72. Cf. Popkin, *Isaac La Peyrère*, chaps. 4, 7.

73. Thomas Hobbes, *Leviathan*, bk. 3, of *The English Works of Thomas Hobbes* (London: Bohn, 1839), chap. 33, pp. 267–68.

74. Ibid.

75. Cf. Popkin, *La Peyrère*, chaps. 4–5.

76. Ibid., chap. 4. The quotation is from La Peyrère's *Men Before Adam* ([London], 1656), p. 208.

77. Popkin, *La Peyrère*, chap. 4, esp. p. 47ff.

78. Ibid., pp. 52–59; and La Peyrère, "Synopsis," in *Du Rappel des Juifs* (n.p., 1643), bk. 4 of *Men Before Adam*.

79. Popkin, *History of Scepticism*, chap. 12; and idem, "Spinoza's Earliest Philosophical Years, 1655–1661," *Studia Spinoziana* (forthcoming).

80. R. H. Popkin and Michael Signer, eds., *Spinoza's Earliest Publication? The Hebrew Translation of Margaret Fell's Loving Salutation* (Assen: Van Gorcum, 1987); R. H. Popkin, "Spinoza and Samuel Fisher," *Philosophia* 15 (1985): 219–36; and R. H. Popkin, "Spinoza's Relations with the Quakers in Amsterdam," *Quaker History* 70 (1984): 14–28.

81. Popkin, "Spinoza and Samuel Fisher," pp. 223–30.

82. Samuel Fisher, *Rusticos ad Academicos, in Exercitationibus Expostulatoriis, Apologeticus quatuor. The Rustick's Alarm to the Rabbies; or, The Country Correcting the University, and Clergy, and (not without good cause) Contesting for the Truth, against the Nursing-Mothers, and their Children* (London, 1660) in *The Testimony of Truth Exalted* (n.p., 1679), pp. 56–58.

83. Fisher, *Rusticos ad Academicos*, p. 696, where he asks, "Is the Light in *America* then any more insufficient to lead its Followers to God, than the Light in *Europe, Asia, Africa*, the other three parts of the World. I have ever lookt upon the Light in all men (since I began to look to it in my self) as one and the self-same Light in all where it is." For Spinoza, see *Tractatus Theologico-Politicus* (New York: Dover, 1951), chaps. 13–14.

84. Spinoza, *Tractatus*, chaps. 1–2.

85. Fisher was attacking the theory of religious knowledge presented by the vice-chancellor of Oxford, John Owen, in his *Reason of Faith* and many other works. On this, see Popkin, "Spinoza and Samuel Fisher," pp. 224–25.

86. *The Confession of Faith, together with the Larger and Lesser Catechismes. Composed by the Reverand Assembly of Divines sitting at Westminster, Presented to both Houses of Parliament* (London, 1658), p. 6.

87. Spinoza, *Tractatus*, chap. 12.

88. Fisher, *Rusticos ad Academicos*, pp. 522–23.

89. Richard Simon, *A Critical History of the Old Testament* (London, 1682), "The Authour's Preface."

90. Cf. R. H. Popkin, "1688 and the Deists in England," in *From Persecution to Toleration*, ed. O. P. Grell, J. I. Israel, N. Tyacke (Oxford: Clarendon Press, 1991), pp. 195–215.

91. Søren Kierkegaard, title page and "Interlude" in *Philosophical Fragments: or, A Fragment of Philosophy* (Princeton: Princeton University Press, 1948), pp. 59–73.

92. On Marlowe, see Paul Kocher, *Christopher Marlowe: A Study of His Thought, Learning, and Character* (New York: Russell & Russell, 1962).

93. Johann Christoph Wagenseil, *Tela ignae Satanae* (Altdorf, 1681); and Johann Jacob Schudt, *Judische Merchwurdigkeiten* (Frankfurt and Leipzig, 1714).

94. The full Latin text is Jean Bodin, *Colloquium heptaplomeres*, ed. Ludovicus Noack (Schwerin, 1857). There is an English translation, *Colloquium of the Seven About Secrets of the Sublime*, trans. and ed. Marion L. Daniels Kuntz (Princeton: Princeton University Press, 1975), and an edition of a French translation, *Colloque entre sept scavans*, ed. François Berriot (Geneva: Droz, 1984).

95. On all of this, see François Berriot, "Avant propos" to Bodin, *Colloque*, pp. xxiv–xxxiv; and R. H. Popkin, "The Dispersion of Bodin's Dialogues in England, Holland, and Germany," *Journal of the History of Ideas* 49 (1988): 157–60.

96. See the "Répertoire des copies manuscrites du *Colloquium hepta-plomeres* ou de *Collogue des secrets cachez*," given by Berriot, in *Collogue*, pp. li–lx.

97. Popkin, "The Role of Jewish Anti-Christian Arguments in the Development of Atheism," in *Atheism from the Reformation to the Enlightenment*, ed. Michael Hunter and David Wootton (Oxford: Oxford University Press, forthcoming).

98. The debate was published by van Limborch under the title *De Veritate religionis christinae: Amico collatio cum erudito Judaeo* (Gouda, 1687). See Locke's correspondence with van Limborch on the debate in 1687 and the review of the debate in the *Bibliothèque universelle* 7 (1687): 289–330, which is most probably by Locke.

99. On Orobio's career, see Yosef Kaplan, *From Christianity to Judaism: The Life and Work of Isaac Orobio de Castro* (New York: Oxford University Press, 1989) (first published in Hebrew [Jerusalem: Magnes Press, 1982]); and R. H. Popkin, "Orobio de Castro," *Encyclopedia Judaica*, vol. 12, cols. 1475–77.

100. Isaac Orobio de Castro, "Prevenciones contra vana idolatria de las gentes" (unpublished). See also, a shorter work by Orobio de Castro, *La Observancia de la Divina Ley de Mosseh*, ed. M. B. Amzalak (Coimbra: Imprensa da Universidad, 1925).

101. Cf. H. P. Salomon's recent edition of Saul Levi Mortera's *Tratado da Verdade da Lei de Moises* (Braga, 1988).

102. Orobio de Castro, Hs. EH 48 E 42, Ets Haim Library, Amsterdam, on the flyleaf.

103. H. P. Salomon has published Mortera's most significant work and intends to publish the rest of his writings. It is hoped that Orobio de Castro's works and others of the Jewish community of the time will be published before long.

104. On this, see R. H. Popkin, "Jacques Basnage's *Histoire des Juifs* and the Biblioteca Sarraziana," *Studia Rosenthaliana* 21 (1987): 154–62.

105. See the article on English by Walter L. Wright, Jr., in the *Dictionary of American Biography*, 3:165, as well as George Bethune English, *The Grounds of Christianity Examined by Comparing the New Testament with the Old* (Boston: Printed for the Author, 1813).

106. [Orobio de Castro], *Israel vengé; ou, Exposition naturelle des Prophéties Hébraïques que les Chrétiens appliquent à Jésus, leur prétendu Messie* (London, 1770).

107. See the notes in the copy of [Orobio de Castro], *Israel vengé*,

Bibliothèque Nationale, Res. D2.5193.

108. See my "1688 and the Deists in England," in *From Persecution to Toleration*, ed. Grell et al.

109. Spinoza, *Tractatus*, chaps. 13–14.

110. This was the view of Charles Blount, John Toland, and Matthew Tindal, the main English deists.

111. Much research is going on concerning the history of this work. Silvia Berti is publishing a critical edition. New information about the work has appeared in several studies by François Charles-Daubert, Silvia Berti, Miguel Benitez, Bertram Schwartzbach, myself, and other scholars. A seminar was held on the sources and origins of the work and the dispersion of its manuscripts at Leiden in summer 1990, sponsored by the Foundation for Research in Intellectual History and conducted by R. H. Popkin, Silvia Berti, Françoise Charles-Daubert, and others. The results will be published in the near future.

112. See esp. Søren Kierkegaard, *Philosophical Fragments* and *Training in Christianity* (Princeton: Princeton University Press, 1967).

113. See Ernest R. Sandeen, *The Roots of Fundamentalism* (Chicago: University of Chicago Press, 1970); David S. Katz, *Sabbath and Sectarianism in Seventeenth-Century England* (Leiden: Brill, 1988), esp. chap. 6; and R. H. Popkin, "*The Age of Reason* Versus *The Age of Revelation*: Two Critics of Tom Paine: David Levi and Elias Boudinot," in *Deism, Masonry, and the Enlightenment: Essays Honoring Alfred Owen Aldridge*, ed. J. A. Leo Lemay (New York: University of Delaware Press, 1987), pp. 158–70.

114. See Sara Kochav, "The Society for Promoting Christianity Among the Jews," Ph.D. diss., Oxford University, 1989; and Leroy E. Froom, *The Prophetic Faith of Our Fathers* (Washington, D.C.: Review and Herald Press, 1946), vols. 2–3.

115. Cf. R. H. Popkin, "Rabbi Nathan Shapira's Visit to Amsterdam in 1657," in *Dutch Jewish History*, ed. J. Michman and T. Levie (Jerusalem: Hebrew University, 1984), pp. 185–205.

116. On Moses Germanus, see Isaac Broydé, "Spaeth, Johann Peter (Moses Germanus)" in *Jewish Encyclopedia*, 2: 483–84; and Reuven Michel, "Spaeth, Johann Peter," in *Encyclopedia Judaica*, vol. 15, col. 219–20. See also, R. H. Popkin, "Spinoza, a Neo-Platonic Kabbalist?" *Proceedings of the International Conference on Jewish Neo-Platonism, Hawaii, 1987*, ed. Lenn Goodman (forthcoming).

CONCLUDING REACTIONS

William P. Alston

First, I want to thank my fellow contributors for their penetrating contributions to the topic. I have, I hope and trust, learned from them.

I will concentrate my remarks on the essays of Audi and Penelhum. That by no means implies any derogation of Popkin's illuminating exploration of the religious and antireligious uses of skepticism in the modern period. Quite the contrary. I very much appreciate his insights. It is just that, lacking any strong temptations to skepticism, I am able to make less use of his work in my own thinking than is the case with the other participants. I will only point out that if one were to defend a "creedless" religious orientation such as Popkin hints at, a great deal would need to be done over and above pointing out the history of its development in certain prominent thinkers.

Let me begin my remarks on Audi and Penelhum by pointing out a fundamental difference between my contribution to this volume and theirs. To put it most simply, where they are concerned with the justification (rationality) of religious belief, I am concerned with knowledge. On the externalist theory of knowledge I expound in my essay I am not concerned with the issues that preoccupy them in their essays. They include such issues as the following: (1) What reason does one have for supposing one's system of religious beliefs to be superior to certain other conflicting systems? (2) How can we show that experience can provide justification for certain beliefs (faith) about God? (3) What is the rational position to take on certain controverted religious issues? I do not mean to suggest that I am not concerned with such issues. On the contrary, I have thought about them long and hard and written about them at some length. I will not attempt to rehash all that, except where it becomes necessary in my critical remarks on Audi and Penelhum. The present point is that on the externalist account of knowledge I defend in my essay, one can have knowledge of God even if one is unable to give satisfactory answers to questions like those just mentioned. And so my essay should be seen as complementary to those of Audi and Penelhum, rather than as opposed, at least in any direct fashion.

To turn to Penelhum, I would first like to express gratification at his agreement with me that our experience of God can provide prima facie justification for certain beliefs about God. And to continue the mutual support, I certainly agree with him that the fact of religious pluralism poses serious problems for the attempt to find a support in experience for religious beliefs. I have attempted to deal with this problem in a recent essay.[1] I also agree with Penelhum that a successful natural theology would be very helpful here. I will add that it would still be very helpful even if its success were measured by less extravagant standards than those often applied in the past. It would not have to proceed solely from premises that would be accepted on reflection by all rational human beings. It would not have to establish its conclusion by deductive reasoning from its premises. Where it provides an explanation, it would not have to show that all conceivable alternative explanations are inferior. Even if it merely provides significant grounds for believing that, for example, the physical universe owes its existence to, and is under the control of, an omnipotent and perfectly good agent, that would be of immense importance. However, I do feel that Penelhum overstates the case when he suggests that a successful natural theology would "disambiguate our world" religiously. The trouble is that many of the most important points that divide religions fall outside the scope of natural theology, at least as it has usually been construed. Could natural theology conceivably tell us that God is revealed to us most fully in the history of Israel and in the life and work of Jesus Christ and of the Christian church? I think not, and I am joined in this opinion by practically all practitioners of natural theology. That enterprise, if successful, might help us to choose between theistic religions and, say, Zen Buddhism, but it has little to say about the choice between different theistic religions. Therefore, while fully agreeing that the enterprise is of the first importance, I would enter a caveat against unrealistic expectations.

One minor quibble with Penelhum before turning to Audi. In the course of his generally admirable historical discussion of various positions on commonsense beliefs and religious beliefs, he has this to say about Reid's response to Hume:

> He [Reid] tells essentially the same story as Hume about the place of commonsense beliefs in our natures but supposes he is refuting the skepticism of Hume by calling the natural beliefs forms of knowledge. Any justification for this dogmatic move comes from his view that the nature with which we are endowed has been given us by God; this claim, however, seems to depend in his system on the very Design Argument that Hume refuted in the *Dialogues*.

Leaving aside the controversial issue of just what Hume did or did not refute in the *Dialogues*, I submit that this grossly misrepresents Reid's critique of Humean skepticism. That is an argument with many prongs, of which I will mention only one, since my own essay provides a starting point for doing so. In the long quotation from Reid in my paper, he is setting out his "undue partiality" argument against Hume. The argument is that Hume (along with Descartes and innumerable others) has taken some of our basic belief-forming propensities uncritically, while refusing to extend the same courtesy to others; and he has no rational basis for this partiality. This is just an example of the way Reid subjects the positions and arguments of his opponents to a searching internal criticism. There is much more to it than Penelhum would lead us to believe.

As for Audi's wide-ranging and synoptic portrayal of the territory of faith, I cannot attempt to comment on nearly all of his important suggestions. I will want to digest much of this over a long time. Here I will confine myself to two matters.

One of Audi's central points is that what he calls "propositional faith" does not necessarily involve or require what he calls "flat-out belief," though he does recognize that they are not incompatible. (One can both have faith that *p* and flat-out believe that *p*.) He obviously takes propositional faith to be in the same ballpark as "flat-out belief." They are both propositional attitudes that guide behavior in the same way (roughly involving a disposition to act as if the proposition is true), both can be more or less rational, and so on. He leaves it rather mysterious just what propositional faith *is*. Like some accounts of God, we are told much more of what it is not than of what it is. I would suppose this mystery can be cleared up very simply as follows. So far as I can see, all of Audi's reasons for denying that faith that *p* requires flat-out belief that *p* can be accommodated by distinguishing different degrees of firmness (confidence, subjective certainty) of belief, and denying that faith that p requires a high degree of firmness of belief. Thus, "the closer one comes to having that belief, the less natural it is to speak of faith rather than simply belief" could be understood as "the more firmly one believes that *p* the less natural it is to speak of faith that *p*." Again, the point that "faith that *p*, as compared with belief that *p*, is compatible with a higher degree of doubt that *p*" invites a similar reading. Thus we might take Audi as saying (or replace his remarks by saying) that faith that *p* can be construed as belief that *p*, together with a positive attitude toward *p*, where the belief can be of any degree of firmness, with the proviso that 'faith that *p*' is used more felicitously where the degree of firmness is significantly below the maximum. That would render the account less mysterious.

Second, I will comment on Audi's discussion of "experiential justification." He begins by setting aside "mystical experience, understood as the rapturous overpowering kind vividly described by William James in *The Varieties of Religious Experience*." He goes on to say: "There is a way to argue for the possibility of direct justification of certain religious beliefs, without presupposing any sources of justification beyond the classically recognized ones that produce foundational beliefs: reason and experience—roughly, intuition and reflection on the one side, and, on the other, sensory experience, introspective consciousness, and memorial impressions . . . This experientialism grounds the justification of some very important religious beliefs in common kinds of experience. Religious people sometimes say that, in ordinary life, God speaks to them, they are aware of God in the beauty of nature, and they can feel God's presence." He then proceeds to consider the epistemic prospects of such an experientialism. I certainly agree that the kinds of putative experiences of God Audi mentions should be given careful consideration. But before setting aside all putative experience of God that does not come through the canonical sources just listed, a couple of questions should be addressed. Why suppose that only the sources listed "produce foundational beliefs"? Audi suggests no more than an argument from authority—the authority, presumably, of epistemologists with whom he agrees. Perhaps a really probing investigation of why we should suppose that these are sources of justified belief would provide us with reasons for supposing that nonsensory putative experiences of God have the same status.[2] Second, I would deny that "rapturous overpowering" experiences (not that there is anything dubious or second rate about such experiences) are the only alternatives to those that are limited to "classically recognized" sources. Many people who think that "they can feel God's presence" take themselves to do so in a nonsensory way even though the experiences are not always "rapturous" and "overpowering."[3] Lest this begins to look like a mere quibble, the important point here is that if we are to give "experientialism" a fair shot, we should take seriously, at the outset, all the ways in which people have taken themselves to be directly aware of God in their experience.

Robert Audi

It is well known that skepticism has profoundly influenced philosophy. Many philosophers have developed their positions as a response to skeptical challenges, and even when philosophers are not addressing skepticism explicitly, it often shapes their thinking. The philosophy of religion is no exception to these points. There are strong rationalist responses to skepticism; the ontological argument is a paradigm. There are experientialist responses; the view that God is in some way encountered in human experience is a common strand in many of them. There are also various fideist responses; here the skeptic is viewed more as an enemy to be vanquished than as an interlocutor to be resisted by counterevidence or persuaded by argument. These and kindred responses to skepticism share a sense that skepticism is a destructive force which must be overcome. There are a few philosophers who, often in the spirit of Hume, think that on many points skepticism may well be right and that, in any case, it need not cast a shadow over the life of the mind and spirit. That we do not or cannot know the truth need not spoil the quest of it and may, in fact, have the benefit of keeping false gods at bay.

The rationalist response to skepticism in the philosophy of religion is in most quarters out of favor, and none of the contributors suggests it as a promising approach. I would deny that proof is the only possible route to knowledge of God. Moreover, at least two among us, Professor Alston and I, have stressed that one can know something without knowing that one does, justifiedly believe something without having justification for believing one does, and, more generally, have a well-grounded propositional attitude without having, or even having grounds for, a higher-order attitude concerning its epistemic status. This bears directly on the rationalist response to skepticism. A major motivation for that response is to provide argumentation which enables us not only to know that God exists but to be warranted in asserting, against the skeptic, that we know this. Again, the ontological argument is a paradigm. It not only (purportedly) proves, but, if successful, can be seen a priori to prove, that God exists. However, once we realize that we can know something even if we cannot show the skeptic that we do, then, quite properly, we are less inclined to think of arguments for God's existence as crucial for the rationality of religious commitment.

These remarks must not be taken to suggest that this volume lacks a defense of the possibility of both knowledge and justified beliefs about God. Working from his own blend of reliabilism and internalism, Alston develops what I would call an experientialist response to skepticism. He argues that experience can ground such knowledge and belief in ways analogous to its production of perceptual knowledge. The question of whether we actually have theistic knowledge and justified belief, like the counterpart question for perception, is not purely philosophical; for philosophical arguments alone cannot show that a cognitive faculty, such as perception, is reliable. Indeed, there is no way to show that, apart from using the faculty itself. Thus, if experience yields knowledge of God, *that* it does so cannot be determined a priori and can be known only through experience itself. But (as I understand Alston) religious experience—which, as he notes, is by no means limited to mystical varieties—is no worse off than ordinary perceptual experience on this point; and if God could create the latter as a reliable source of knowledge of the external world, God could equally well create the former as a reliable source of knowledge of religious truths.

In Professor Penelhum's essay, I find less optimism about meeting the skeptical challenge to the view that religious commitment can be rational. It is not that Penelhum regards arguments for God's existence as needed here and finds them wanting. Far from it. He is not here concerned with those arguments and recognizes much plausibility in what he aptly calls the Basic Belief Apologetic due especially to Plantinga, Alston, Wolterstorff, and others. But suppose that this experientialist response to skepticism is sound. It still establishes only parity among the various differing religious outlooks for which experience yields the appropriate theistic confirmation. How can it be rational for me to accept my religious views when others with equally confirmatory experiences of the same sort hold religious views incompatible with mine? If our grounds are equally good, why conclude that we are equally rational rather than equally *ir*rational? It is here that Penelhum sees an important role for natural theology. A sound natural theology would serve to disambiguate our experience. As I understand it, this might enable religious people to preserve those of their religious beliefs that receive sufficient support from the relevant natural considerations and to revise or give up those representing only cultural preferences or mere prejudices. Penelhum does not commit himself regarding the likelihood of anyone's working out such a theology; but, in my view, an important implication of his essay is that the Basic Belief Apologetic should not be allowed to obscure the importance of natural theology in the general project of reconciling faith and reason.

Where Alston sees the skeptic as vanquished—or at any rate repulsed—and Penelhum takes skepticism to be a continuing threat to the view that religious commitment can be rational, Professor Popkin is quite hospitable to a healthy skepticism. He notes that, as Hume saw, one can be a skeptic about a view yet still not suspend judgment on it; and he stresses that certain religious views may be held quite compatibly with skepticism regarding their truth. One can, for instance, hold a creedless faith; this is not an outlook without content, but one not tied to traditional dogmas nor taken to represent knowledge. Popkin even sees skepticism as "cleansing." As I interpret him, he takes it to undermine dogma—and dogmatism—and to help in keeping us open to intellectual and spiritual renewal. A substantial degree of confirmation of this view of skepticism can be found in a number of the historical case studies that his paper recounts.

My own effort is to clarify the rationality of religious commitment as a whole, including its behavioral as well as cognitive dimensions, and to do so in a way that reduces the threat of skepticism. Let me first sketch the central notion I work with and then proceed to the epistemological results of so doing.

My initial strategy is to outline a religiously significant notion of a kind of faith which, because it has propositional objects —such as that God is sovereign—is cognitive, and, because it does not imply unqualifiedly believing these propositions, is nondoxastic. Such faith is, however, by and large cognitively stronger than hope, always incompatible with disbelieving its propositional object, and fully compatible with an attitude of steadfast confidence and trust. I suggest that such faith can be sufficiently rich in content, and attitudinally strong enough, to ground the behavioral and attitudinal commitments appropriate to a religious life. It can encompass the appropriate doctrines, unify the required attitudes of reverence and piety, and motivate the appropriate religious and moral behavior.

The epistemological significance of taking nondoxastic faith as a central religious attitude can be seen by reflecting on the difference between the conditions for the rationality (or the justification) of a hope that p as opposed to a flat-out belief that p. The grounds for, say, rationally hoping that it will rain are far weaker than those for flatly believing that it will. While I certainly do not deny that hope is religiously important, I take even nondoxastic faith to be stronger. Other things being equal, it implies a higher degree of what we might call *cognitive inclination* toward the relevant proposition. But it is nonetheless weaker, in its purely cognitive dimension, than flat-out belief. With the latter, we have something like cognitive embrace. Corresponding to this distinction in the cognitive dimension is an epistemic difference: The rationality conditions for nondoxastic faith are less stringent than those for flatly believing the same proposition. To be sure, even with respect to nondoxastic faith the skeptic can make a case against rationality (or, especially, justification, which my paper distinguishes from rationality); but the case is surely weaker than its counterpart for flat-out religious belief. It may be, then, that if some of the discussion of the rationality of cognitive religious commitment is redirected toward nondoxastic faith as opposed to belief, a new and perhaps better appraisal of skepticism can be accomplished.

If nondoxastic fiduciary attitudes are taken to be religiously central in the way I suggest they can be in some religious lives, then there are a few points of comparison and contrast with the other contributors to this volume that deserve brief mention. My views can best be brought out if I address the essays by Penelhum, Alston, and Popkin in that order.

The parity problem raised by Penelhum remains for my view, but seems less serious than for accounts in which belief is the central focus of religious commitment. If others have equally well-grounded (nondoxastic) religious faith with propositional objects incompatible with the truth of one's own faith, this is certainly a prima facie reason to wonder whether one might be in error or might at least need to seek further grounds. But there is no good reason to doubt that one's faith is rational simply because someone else with equally good grounds has faith with incompatible content. I do not deny that the same might be said about religious belief; but if I am correct in holding that rationality there requires stronger grounds, the problem is at least more serious in that case, since, other things being equal, the stronger one takes one's grounds to be, the more concerned one should be upon discovering others who, on the basis of equally good grounds, hold incompatible beliefs.

Like Alston, I am conceiving knowledge in a largely externalistic way. It represents, above all, an epistemic success, whether it is achieved by an internally accessible route or not. But unlike him I am conceiving rationality and justification in an essentially internalist way. I have no difficulty, then, with the view, implicit in externalism as applied to divine capacities, that God might endow us with faculties capable of reliably producing theistic beliefs. But I do not take it as obvious that there is or can be an internally accessible route, such as an a priori argument, to rational theistic (flat-out) belief. There might, on the other hand, be a perceptual route, as Alston and others have argued (in works cited in his essay). But if there is, it is not quite plain to me (for reasons given in my essay) that it can sustain the rationality of theistic beliefs. I leave this open. In any case, it might still sustain the rationality of faith. Whether it does or not, the epistemic requirements for its success in sustaining the rationality of faith are less stringent than those governing success in grounding the rationality of flat-out belief.

With Popkin, I share a sense of the positive value of skepticism, but I am less comfortable with skepticism than he is. I completely agree with him that one can hold a view while also being skeptical regarding one's grounds for it. It may be worth emphasizing that proponents of the Basic Belief Apologetic can also accept this point. But whereas (despite Hume's insight to the contrary) many skeptics tend to think that it cannot be rational to hold a view while believing one lacks good grounds for it, one could adhere to much of the Basic Belief Apologetic and still believe this. One could certainly claim that through epistemological error (or lack of faith) one who never even wavers in one's religious convictions can hold the second-order view that they represent sheer faith and are not "rationally justified." Part of the thrust of the Basic Belief Apologetic is to bring out that even if one has no evidence or arguments for religious beliefs, one may still have grounds. Skepticism can obscure this point, for it preoccupies us with giving evidence and easily creates the impression that our grounds for a view are no better than the evidences we can marshall in argumentative self-defense. But even though this impression is mistaken, the self-defensive effort can be cleansing and illuminating. Popkin is surely right about that effect of skepticism, and a faith that survives a clash with skepticism may be both attitudinally stronger and doctrinally better than one never subjected to skeptical scrutiny.

Perhaps there is no refuting skepticism, at least about knowledge and belief concerning God; but if not, it may still be possible to rebut such skepticism, in the sense of showing that its arguments are unsound. Certainly the negative task of revealing defects in skeptical arguments need not wait upon the positive task of establishing that we actually have the knowledge and justified beliefs skeptics deny we possess. Similarly, the rationality of religious commitment should not be conceived as exhausted by the potential antiskeptical arguments underlying it. And if I have been right, the rationality of that commitment should not be conceived—even in its purely cognitive dimensions—as wholly a matter of the grounds of religious beliefs. Faith as a distinctive attitude may also carry that commitment; its rationality is subject to lesser constraints; and its reconciliation with reason in the lives of the religious should be approached in the light of their overall experience: cognitive, emotional, perceptual, and spiritual. Some lives contain far more than others in the way of grounds for religious commitment. It is essential to grasp—as recent literature has established—that not all of these grounds are evidential and that some are experiential in a way not unlike the grounds of perceptual belief; but it is also important to realize—as the literature has neglected to bring out—that the various grounds apply differentially to faith and belief.

Terence Penelhum

In my essay I attempted to make use of some facts in the history of philosophy to reveal the limitations of an influential form of apologetic developed in recent years. I see these limitations as being due to the fact that we live in a culture that presents us with too many viable religious and secular choices. That is to say, we each confront a bewildering variety of worldviews and life-options, each of which appears to be defensible and to be certifiable as rational by this form of apologetic argument, although it has been offered as a specific defense of the Christian faith. I see the role of natural theology as that of addressing this multiple ambiguity in our world; and if it is a role that cannot be discharged, Christians (and indeed all theists) have a problem in the very fact of ambiguity itself.

While our own era presents this distinctive array of alternatives to the reflective person, I do not wish to exaggerate its distinctiveness. The sheer variety of intellectual options, each capable of support, was a feature of the world to which the classical skeptic responded; and the fear of the same rational pluralism was one of the primary sources of those fideisms of the early modern period that Richard Popkin has illuminated so much for us. My own reflections on this tradition would have been quite impossible without this illumination, and I am grateful for the additional riches and insights he has made available to us here. I shall confine my comments to the noncredal faith that he commends as the best response to skeptical perplexities.

From the historical examples he gives, I judge this noncredal faith to combine an openness to religious experience with a Judeo-Christian ethic but to be free of doctrinal commitments and institutional forms. This stance is of course different from the conformist social religion of a Sextus, but this would be expected in the different religious environment of the seventeenth century. What the early modern period in Europe did ensure, however, was that an attempt at a noncredal religious life would take an overtly or tacitly theistic form, that religious experience would be taken to be experience of God, and that a religious humanism would be a humanism based on a shared theistic assumption of creatureliness. In the late twentieth century, we cannot fail to be aware that the most strongly mystical traditions of the world are nontheistic and that any shared perceptions of humanity that are common to them and to the Jew, Christian, or Moslem, will have to be articulated in a language that is neutral on this most fundamental religious matter. I am not certain that the efforts of scholars (such as Wilfred Cantwell Smith and John Hick) to introduce a suitably ecumenical religious vocabulary have been successful so far. But however this may be, I doubt whether a sufficiently nondoctrinal religious stance is possible unless it centers on a spirituality that is mystical in the strict sense of cultivating a contemplative experience that is ineffable and beyond any descriptive denominators common to the Western theistic religions. I suspect that what Popkin commends is a religious stance that is at most relatively creedless—one that implies a creed that is short but not nonexistent. Such a form would be much less nearly universalistic than he says.

Someone seeking faith in a religiously ambiguous world is

bound to be attracted to an understanding of what faith requires that is like the one Robert Audi offers us. So I very much regret finding a difficulty in it. If I understand him correctly, he distinguishes between the doxastic and attitudinal aspects of faith, and he argues that one can have faith without one's doxastic position amounting to what he calls flat-out belief. What is necessary is rather that one have some significant degree of belief (or of inclination to belief) and that this be combined with a proper attitudinal stance—one in which the subject is prepared to base his or her life and conduct on that which he or she inclines to believe to be true. It is not surprising that Audi shows sympathy to analyses of faith that treat its doxastic component as similar to hope. The stance he describes may well be the best that many, or even any, putative believers in our day can rise to. But I see a problem in the way of holding that this is what faith is. I take him to be offering it as a possible form of Christian faith. Any analysis of this has to fit the paradigms of faith that we find in the New Testament. Among these are the states of mind commended as faith by Jesus in the Gospels. It is striking that these consist, for the most part, in a serene confidence that what is requested of him will come to pass if he consents. Absence of intellectual hesitation may not be a sufficient condition of such serenity (for those who are rebuked because their faith is too little seem to fail because their knowledge of God's care does not issue in freedom from anxiety, not because they do not believe in his care); but it does seem to be a necessary condition. For if one has doubts about someone, yet trusts that person in spite of them, this trust is of the kind that is based on deliberate resolution (like the kind a probation officer shows a parolee or a driving instructor shows a pupil). It does not seem to be this deliberate trust that the Gospels commend as faith. Perhaps one must say that the stance Audi describes can be a stage on the way to the real thing.

William Alston's reliabilist account of religious knowledge is not offered as an exercise in apologetics. But his impressive argument does have apologetic implications, and I shall confine my comment to these. It is, from one view, a great apologetic strength to have a view of knowledge that enables you to say that a person's beliefs can amount to knowledge if they are arrived at by mechanisms that are reliable ways toward truth, even if the person who has those beliefs and has acquired them in this way is in no position to establish or defend the reliability of those mechanisms. Such a view coincides with the perennial Christian insistence that God has revealed himself to the simple rather than the wise, as Alston says. From that same point of view it is a further strength, though I think a lesser one, that this analysis of knowledge makes the identification of reliable ways to truth an empirical matter, to be settled by those conversant with the subject. The question this leaves, sometimes easy and sometimes hard, is that of how this community is itself to be identified. Alston briskly identifies it with theologians. While this could be disputed by unbelievers who would offer their own substitute experts, such as psychologists, I do not wish to follow them. I see a more difficult problem when one considers the claims of the authorities of religious traditions other than one's own, and the supposed knowledge that the nonexpert adherents of those traditions think they have. The apologetic difficulty one faces here is part of the difficulty that concerned me in my own essay: Alston's analysis is one that would permit those of other traditions to accept it and to offer their own claims as examples of reliably acquired beliefs. I emphasize that this obvious point is not intended as an objection to Alston's position. I merely point out that the limitation I claimed to find in the Basic Belief Apologetic is one that would remain if his analysis of knowledge, which is clearly intended to be complementary to it, were accepted.

Richard H. Popkin

In reading the other essays, I feel that I am the odd man out, since I am not an analytic philosopher, I am not a Christian, and I am a skeptic and a mystic. In all these respects, I find myself apart from the concerns of the other contributors. Each of them carefully and elegantly has sought to show, on analytic philosophical standards, that one does not have to declare religious beliefs, or propositions that state them, to be meaningless, worthless, unverifiable, and so forth. The epistemological analysis of an acceptable criterion of reliability of beliefs and of rational or reasonable evidence for accepting basic beliefs, according to the other contributors, could or should lead to the acceptability of some religious propositions.

It seems to me that a wrong turn was taken in the philosophy of religion and as a result of Hume's skeptical examination of evidence for asserting the existence of God or identifying any attributes of the Divine Being. Hume centered the question on evidence, and he associated so-called religious experience with bizarre psychological behavior. One reason for this may be Hume's frank avowal to Frances Hutcheson that when he thought of the idea of God, nothing followed. The idea left him cold, without any associated ideas or feelings. (And, for Hume, feelings are beliefs, and vice versa.)

I can deal with intellectual issues only by placing them in their historical contexts. Hence, as a historian, I sought to show how the skeptical fideism of Montaigne, Charron, Pascal, and the quietists became a skepticism *against* religion by applying evidential standards to basic religious beliefs. Before Hume came on the scene, it had been obvious to the intellectually astute devout that the application of the evidential standards that developed from Descartes onward should not be applied to religious principles. Bishop Edward Stillingfleet attacked Locke because he saw that the application of Locke's empirical theory of knowledge to religious belief (by John Toland, not by Locke) would lead to the denial of all serious principles of the Christian religion. Stillingfleet diagnosed the future course of the understanding and evaluation of religion by deists, agnostics, and atheists.

Pierre Bayle's most orthodox opponent, Pierre Jurieu, the leader of the French Protestants in the Netherlands, insisted that one of the most dangerous heresies was that one should only believe propositions only if they are clear and distinct. He had the

Cartesian criterion condemned at a synod of the French Reformed church in 1692 because it would undermine religious belief.

Stillingfleet and Jurieu were believers. Hume said what they said, as an unbeliever, and made the result seem startling and exciting and antireligious.

But, I think, it is only startling, exciting, and irreligious if one has made belief an evidential matter. The key problem of natural theology, as presented by Penelhum, is to prove the existence of God. But, who needs a proof or wants a proof? From Augustine and Anselm onward, God's existence is the core of faith, and the proof only arises for faith seeking understanding or for someone who has no faith.

Perhaps my own personal starting point makes me suspicious of the kind of evidential search involved in the other three essays, suspicious because the evidential search seems to yield little in itself. Then we are told that maybe, if we worked harder and harder at it, we might prove something of religious interest or of interest to religious people. But it seems to me that people who have direct religious experience do not need further evidence. In fact, evidential questions are irrelevant, since the experience is self-revealing and self-validating; that is, anyone who has such experiences knows that he or she has them and knows they need nothing else to validate them as religious experiences. In fact, evidence, as Pascal said, is never enough to justify belief or disbelief. Religious experience stands by itself and does not need a "justifiable" or "reliable" belief system to support it.

The significant questions for the person with direct religious experience, the mystic, are how to interpret the experience and how to relate it to other kinds of experiences. And here we might come to evidential problems. Is the experience related to the claims of any particular religious tradition? The three other contributors to this volume are Christians and seem to take it for granted that religious belief is Christian belief. As a nonChristian, a Jew, I do not find Christianity a live option, insofar as Christianity is presented as the fulfillment of Judaism. Hence, the scriptural or empirical evidence that Christianity is true and Judaism is false, the basis for discussions that fascinated theologians from early Christianity onward, does not impress me. All of the data adduced on either side are open to many interpretations. Hence, the natural theology or just plain theology offered by the others seems to beg the question of what is appropriate data. To tell theology from mythology seems to me to require some religious data to start with. How does one get from religious experience to religious data?

Every person who has religious experience, I think, seeks to put it in some human context–an ongoing religious tradition, a collection of symbols, and so forth. Since I find no particular reason why religious experience, as I have encountered it personally, should be placed in one tradition or another, I am a religious pluralist. Each believer has to decide for herself or himself how to interpret the experience, and what data to connect it with. In so deciding, I think William James's notion of a living option is relevant. My religious experiences led me, and made me, look into my own tradition, of which I was quite ignorant at the time. It led me to a broad tolerance of other traditions but not to any personal concern about them. I found myself thrust into Jewish history, as both a living and a forced option.

My skepticism kept me from any dogmatic or monistic interpretation. I became interested in those thinkers in the seventeenth and eighteenth centuries who developed a creedless religion beyond both Judaism and Christianity and developed this *after* setting forth a total Pyrrhonism. They advocated recognizing a religious center of meaning, being, and action, without attaching this to any particular historical formulation and set of activities. It is somewhat like the explanation of Judaism given by Rabbi Hillel in the first century. He was asked to explain Judaism while standing on one foot. He is reported to have said, "Do not unto others as you would have them not do unto you. All the rest is commentary."

The analysis and evaluation of evidence for religious belief is a new form of commentary that develops from Hume onward.

Instead of the evidences that were offered for Judaism and Christianity by apologists like Saul Levi Mortera, Orobio de Castro, Hugo Grotius, and Blaise Pascal, one now offers disproofs of arguments for agnosticism and atheism. This can be of importance if the discussion of where this leaves us is rooted in living religious experience. Without such a basis, I find that no matter how carefully one analyzes the bases of reasonable belief, of kinds of evidences, no particular religious conclusion will result. My colleagues end their essays with optimistic pictures of what might follow, if one went on to develop natural theology, to evaluate religious knowledge claims, and so forth. But this seems to involve a leap into faith and into one particular faith, Christianity, which I do not find at all justified by their careful analysis of the belief context.

On the other hand, if one starts from living religious experience, then each believer will find what is a live option for herself or himself. And each live option can then be carefully explored and explicated. The result will be meaningful for each believer, though probably quite individualistic and maybe idiosyncratic. The moral and social values of a community of believers may lead the individual believers to group together, without having to curtail or change their beliefs. The historical Jewish communities have been held together by common practices or common values, without the need for common creeds. And two of the leading twentieth-century Jewish theologians or philosophers of Judaism, Martin Buber and Franz Rosenzweig, have emphasized this as a basis for.meaningful faith within the pervasive skepticism of modern times. (And, of course, both have been rejected or ignored by the main institutions of orthodox Judaism.)

Notes

1. "Religious Diversity and the Perceptual Knowledge of God," *Faith and Philosophy* 5 (Oct. 1988), pp. 433–48.

2. I have suggested this move in various publications. See, e.g., "Religious Experience and Religious Belief," *Nous* 16 (1982): 2–12; "Christian

Experience and Christian Belief," in *Faith and Rationality*, ed. Alvin Plantinga and Nicholas Wolterstorff (Notre Dame: University of Notre Dame Press, 1983), pp. 103–34; *Perceiving God: A Study in the Epistemology of Religious Experience* (Ithaca, N.Y.: Cornell University Press, 1991).

3. See my "The Perception of God," *Philosophical Topics* 16 (Fall 1988).

ABOUT THE AUTHORS

William P. Alston is Professor of Philosophy at Syracuse University. He was educated at Centenary College and the University of Chicago. Among his publications are *The Philosophy of Language*, *Epistemic Justification*, *Divine Nature and Human Language*, and *Perceiving God*.

Robert Audi is Professor of Philosophy at the University of Nebraska. He was educated at Colgate University and the University of Michigan. Among his several books are *Rationality, Religious Belief, and Moral Commitment*; *Belief, Justification, and Knowledge*; and *Practical Reasoning*.

Marcus Hester is Professor of Philosophy at Wake Forest University. He was educated at Wake Forest University and Vanderbilt University. Among his publications are *The Meaning of Poetic Metaphor* and *Sensibility and Criticism*.

Terence Penelhum is Professor Emeritus of Religious Studies and former Director of the Institute for the Humanities at the University of Calgary. He was educated at the University of Edinburgh and at Oxford University. Among his many published works are *Survival and Disembodied Existence*, *Religion and Rationality*, and *Problems of Religious Knowledge*.

Richard H. Popkin was Professor of Philosophy at Washington University until he retired from full-time teaching in December 1986. He is now Adjunct Professor of History and Philosophy at the University of California at Los Angeles. Among his books are *The History of Scepticism from Erasmus to Descartes*, *The Second Oswald*, and *The High Road to Pyrrhonism*. He has published over two hundred articles, including many on the history of philosophy and Jewish intellectual history.

INDEX